Hackers Exposed

I0016109

Discover the secret world of cybercrime

FERNANDO UILHERME BARBOSA DE AZEVEDO

Table of Content

About the Author

Fernando Uilherme Barbosa de Azevedo is an electronic, electrical and industrial engineer graduated from Pontifícia Universidade Católica of Rio de Janeiro. He is MBA graduate from Fundação Getúlio Vargas. He has been a programming instructor at Pontifícia Universidade Católica of Rio de Janeiro for 7 years.

He published his first book "Macros for Excel hands on" by publisher Campus/Elsevier at age 27. The book is still sold in Brazil and Portugal.

His first startup business won a prize from the Brazilian Federal Institutional FINEP.

Coming to the United States in 2014, Fernando studied Web Development and Internet Technologies at University of California Santa Cruz - Silicon Valley Extension and also completed the "Innovation and Entrepreneurship Certification" from Stanford University.

Fernando has been featured many times in news media and TV. He was interviewed as a specialist on his field by Forbes, The Entrepreneur, el Nuevo Herald and many other major Brazilian media companies.

Today, Fernando runs 2 internet marketing companies in the United States and has clients in many countries. The companies offer services such as internet marketing, SEO, Online Reputation Managements, pen testing, systems audit, e-commerce, apps and other internet related activities.

He is also a web development instructor for IronHack and weekly speaker at Radio Gazeta.

Fernando considers himself an ethical hacker and thinks that the internet should be a safer place. By advocating against all the unethical activities online that are still present today, he hopes that our leaders and law makers can become aware of these threats and help create laws for a safer world.

This book is dedicated to Fernando's sister Christiane Monnerat.

This book is a series of 5 books related to Internet Technologies and how the internet works. If you like this book, please check out other books from the same author.

Introduction

Hacking is a term that's widely used, but only a few truly understand. What it is and what it really means to "hack" may have several variations with its definitions but to cut most colloquialisms, let's begin by clearing what the *hacking* we're going to be talking about in this book *isn't*. Prominent colloquialisms such as "life hacks" have nothing to do with it, but terms such as malware and phishing, and activities such as device tampering, identity theft, and domain hijacking all belong to the complicated and yet fascinating world and web of hacking.

The term "hacking" generally means the unwanted and often unauthorized intrusion and altering of a computer, a network, or a system. Any computer programmer who can do this is called a *hacker*.

Most people on the internet are scared of hackers, and quite rightfully so. The term hacker usually has a negative connotation tied to it as people connect the word hacker to infamous people on the internet who make weapons of mass chaos using only computer code — something that our ancestors could've never imagined possible.

Hackers thrive in the 21st century, mostly because being a hacker pays. Corporations hire hackers for their ability to use their skills to find security flaws that put vital information on the line; such as a bank, for example, may hire hackers to prevent cyber crimes such as Salami Slicing. Hired hackers also help prevent identity theft, theft in general, and all the other cyber related crimes.

However, it isn't all positive. Hackers can also be hired to do the exact opposite. It seems humans always have a way of abusing whatever innovation exists. With the prominence of cybercrime, within a decade, we'll just call it crime. And the center of it all? Hackers.

Most hackers go by their own alter egos, pseudonyms, and aliases. Just like in the real world, everybody has different identities. Who you are to your mother won't be exactly the same as who you are to your friends. Identities serve as masks and the same concept applies in the cyber world. Everyone can have different aliases and pseudonyms that allow us freedom of expression — and presumably actions without consequences.

The physical disconnection gives people a different sense of reality. It's easier to do things when you're operating in your own home, behind a screen. This makes it seem that the consequences are minimal – or sometimes even absent.

The emergence of darknets and online cryptocurrencies in the modern world have made it an easier world for hackers to move around and do their jobs almost anonymously.

This book will try to uncover some of the secrets that hackers have up their sleeves, in the hopes that not only will people reading this be informed, but also understand what goes on behind cybercrimes. This book will also outline some of the basics of cybercrime and how all of it works; the reasons for committing them, the effects of successful attacks, as well as the precautions to take to avoid being the victim of these attacks. Throughout the book we will also be looking back at the biggest cyber crimes committed in history. System administrators turned into hackers, weapons made completely out of code, and even the "discovery" of hidden information about UFO's. This is Hackers Exposed: A Look into Cyber Crime.

Thank you and I hope you enjoy it!

Chapter 1: Famous Cases

On average, 90% of businesses stated that they experience at least one cyber attack attempt per year. Seventy percent of which is reported to be successful. This statistic is just one study that shows the prominence of cybercrime, but it doesn't show just how powerful hackers behind these crimes might be. Behind these cybercrimes are real people with real stories. Some are just shockingly lucky to land their hands on malicious software that turned out to be powerful, but a good number are also experts in the field of hacking, creating their own virus codes, turning them in weapons of mass destruction, and causing fear with just a click of a button.

In this section, we look at five of the most famous cases in the cybercrime world.

Our first case proves that cybercrime knows no distance, and perhaps no boundaries as well. Vladimir Levin is a name and entity well-known in the 1990's for hacking into several popular websites. His biggest accomplishment, if you'll call it that, was when he gained access to Citibank's bank accounts in 1994. He was able to transfer $10.7 million dollars in different bank accounts that he and accomplices had set up Finland, the United States, the Netherlands, Germany and Israel. Three of the said accomplices, however, were arrested when they tried to withdraw the money in Tel Aviv, Rotterdam and San Francisco in 1995. Interrogations of the 3 accomplices led the law enforcement to Vladimir Levin, then working at AO Saturn, a computer company based in St. Petersburg. It took a while for Levin to be convicted because Russia's Constitution prohibits extradition of its citizens to foreign countries, but in 1998 he was convicted and sentenced to three years in jail, with the addition of paying over $240,000 as restitution. Only $400,000, however, was found and recovered from the millions he has stolen. After serving his 3 years of jail time, he settled down and currently owns and runs a business in Lithuania.

That whole narrative is the common story and it's what most people know, but a revelation surfaced ten years later. In 2005, one of the members of the St. Petersburg hacker group claimed to have been the original penetrators of Citibank. He also revealed that Vladimir Levin wasn't what people thought him to be. He wasn't this super genius mathematician or the like, instead, he was an ordinary system administrator that got his hands on the ready data to penetrate Citibank, reportedly for only $100. The original Citibank penetrators claimed that they played around with Citibank's unprotected systems, examining its structures and noting that none of the bank's staff noticed any suspicious activity. The alleged original penetrators admitted that robbery wasn't in any of their plans, until one of the members of the group reportedly gave over the information to Vladimir Levin. The alleged original penetrators weren't touched by law enforcement, seeing as they didn't actually commit a crime, aside from pointing out that Citibank's security was insufficient. There are also no records — nine identifiable by Citibank's security or the law enforcement, anyway — that show that these group of people ever altered anything in Citibank's systems.

There's no acknowledged universal truth with this story, just that Vladimir Levin had gotten what he deserved in the eyes of the law. Some say thought that for someone who was lucky enough to get his hands on ready data to successfully penetrate a known bank such as Citibank, his short sentence and the restitution was a small price to pay for such rewards of a crime like this.

The more you spend time looking at cybercrime cases, the more you start to notice that banks are big targets for hackers. Especially in the early days of the internet and in the 1990s, bank security was no concern for hackers who knew their craft — or those lucky enough to find data by hackers who knew their craft. These are commonly sold on the black markets of the dark web, and it allows even the most amateur hackers to possibly get their hands on big security breaches.

Another famous, or rather infamous name in the world of cybercrime is Max Ray Butler, also known as the "Ice Man". He was a former security researcher that turned into one of the most notorious cybercriminals. He gained notoriety for hacking into websites that bought and sold stolen credit card numbers. After hacking into these websites, he then forced the buyers and sellers on the hacked site to conduct their businesses on his own site called *Carders Market*. The stolen credit card numbers were used to create fake physical cards that are used to withdraw the money in the accounts or buy merchandise using the accounts. In 2002, Max Ray Butler served an 18-month sentence in prison for the creation of a malicious software that allows hackers to install backdoor programs on computers, as well as government websites. His malware allowed hackers to alter computers and use them for other cyber crimes such as ransomware. The Ice Man was released in the same year but turned back to the world of cybercrime when he severely fell short on money. As mentioned in the introduction of this book, cyber crime *pays*. He was arrested again in September 2007, but before that, he was able to create the biggest marketplace for stolen credit card information in the world. Three years after his arrest, he was sentenced to 13 years in federal prison for all the cyber crimes he has committed, and on top of the sentence he had to pay $2.5 million as restitution for all his victims. Max Ray Butler's 13-year sentence was, at that time, the longest sentence ever given for charges of hacking in the United States. His sentence and the general consequence of his actions are far from Vladimir Levin's 3 years of jail time, but their pay also differed. And the difference was not small. Max Ray Butler stole almost 2 million credit card numbers and earned over $86 million. Vladimir Levin's $10.7 million Citibank attempt seems like merely change next to the Ice Man's stolen money.

Money is one of the major factors that drive people in committing cyber crimes, just as with normal crimes. Money is, however, not the only reason.

The next hacker on the list is Gary McKinnon, a Scottish systems administrator. He was accused of committing one of the most notorious military computer hacks of all time. And yes, you read that right: he was *accused*. There wasn't enough evidence to land Gary McKinnon in jail and the biggest military computer hack might not be fully attributed to him, but it's just too big and too famous of a case to not be included on this list. And what comes as a surprise to many people is that his drive wasn't money.

Gary McKinnon was accused of hacking a total of 97 computers, both from the United States military and NASA, in a span of 13 months. He allegedly used the name "Solo" for all his hacking activities, which was said to have been done at the house of his girlfriend's aunt in London.

After his arrest in March 2002, Gary McKinnon received an indictment in November of the same year. The indictment contained seven criminal counts — all related to cybercrime and each potentially carried ten-year jail time.

Among the seven criminal counts, the US military accused him of immobilizing sensitive systems, as well as deleting and altering files at a US naval air station after the 9/11 terrorist attacks.

What's so impressive and at the same time increasingly scary is that Gary McKinnon used commercially available software. He used these to probe dozens of US military and government networks. According to him, the machines he found had inadequate firewall protection and the absence of passwords, so he simply hacked into them.

He has always stood by his statement that he never acted with the intent to harm. He was no code writer for viruses nor a web vandal. He was merely "researching" to find classified documents about Unidentified Flying Objects or UFOs. He also believed that the United States government had crucial information about the topic and that they were withholding this information from the public, so he used his hacking skills to find the critical information.

What started as a simple interest and investigation, however, quickly became an obsession.

In August of 2008, several psychologists diagnosed Gary McKinnon with Asperger's Syndrome, a developmental disorder characterized by factors including restricted and repetitive patterns of behavior and interest.

The diagnosis was merely a hunch a televised interview of Gary McKinnon was observed by experts in the field. A professor named Simon Baron-Cohen confirmed the hunch, issued an official diagnosis, and said that it was indeed consistent with McKinnon's actions and mentality. He was obsessively searching for what he perceived as the "truth".

He called his hacking activities into the US military and NASA computers a "moral crusade". He believed that he could find actual evidence that intelligence agencies such as NASA had technology from extra-terrestrial beings. He also believed that the technology could be used for good and that NASA shielded it from the world because of selfish reasons. He said that while he was hacking into the systems, he only thought about how unjust the United States was to be shielding that type of information from the world. He claimed to have not thought of the consequences of his actions, especially jail sentences and criminal counts.

Sufferers of Asperger's syndrome are known to have a level of social naiveté when it comes to evaluating the consequences of their actions.

Soon statements from Gary McKinnon more and more added up to his diagnosis of Asperger's syndrome.

Until June 2005, he remained at liberty without restriction. He was facing the possibility of being extradited to the United States and serving up to 70 years in prison and possibly even to the Guantanamo Bay detention camp - where inmates are detained indefinitely without trial.

After passing through several courts and appeals, then-Home Secretary Theresa May announces that his extradition has been blocked on the 16th of October 2012. While Gary McKinnon was facing accusations of serious crimes, he was also suffering from Asperger's syndrome and depressive illnesses. His extradition could risk having him end his own life, and the decision to extradite would be a violation of his human rights.

From Gary McKinnon's case we see the different things that drive people to committing cybercrimes, and it isn't always money. This case also proves that behind the masks, aliases, and personas on the internet, there hackers are still *real people*.

The next on our list of famous cases, however, is no person. Its effects, however, surpassed any of the previously mentioned cybercrimes. On this case we discuss a virus that emerged during the early days of the internet and it took the cyber world by storm. On the 26th of March 1999, American citizen David L. Smith introduced to the world his one and only: the Melissa virus. This macro virus was officially known as W97M/Melissa.A@mm. It might have been David L. Smith's only creation, but it has grown to become one of the world's worst mass-emailing virus ever created.

The virus got its name from an exotic dancer and stripper in Miami, but it's official name, came from the antivirus creators. As a rule, viruses are given no proper names, but this macro virus' name from the creator stuck.

Within hours of its release, the Melissa virus had spread through tens of thousands of computers all over the world. All the infected computers had one factor in common: they all relied on Microsoft Outlook for an email service. This meant all personal computers and even those within government agencies were infected.

It spreads through an email with a Word document attached to it. Before the virus could infect a computer, the attached file must be manually downloaded. This meant that recipient of the email must actually click on the attachment for the virus to infect a computer. David L. Smith knew this and had taken this into account, because he made sure that the recipients of the emails would *want* to open the attachments. He used social engineering, which will be discussed further into the book, to entice his victims to open the email and click the attachment. The emails were from accounts of the victim's friends, families, or colleagues. Many were fooled.

The emails seemed like important messages from people the victim knew, making it more enticing. The subject line would usually say that they're an important message from someone the victim knows. Users can be easily fooled because the virus uses real names that are connected to the users. The sole content of the email would be the attachment and a message that tells the user that the attachment is the document that they asked for, along with a note to not show anyone else. The short message ends with a wink emoticon, making it more enticing and teasing.

The virus was spread during the early days of the internet and there wasn't a lot of people who were properly educated on viruses — or even the existence of them — so a lot of people were easily fooled and clicked the email attachment, allowing Melissa to infect their computers.

So, how does the Melissa virus work and what does it do to the computer it infects? As soon as the attachment, often with the name LIST.DOC, is saved to the computer, it disables several safeguards in Microsoft Word, either the 97 version or the 2000 version. This is made possible because the virus' file has a script from Visual Basic. This script runs and puts the infected file, in the normal.dot used by Microsoft Word as a template for both default and custom settings.

If the user has Microsoft Outlook on their computer as an email program, using the Visual Basic code again, the email containing the attachment and the note is sent to the 50 addresses on top of each victim's Outlook address books found in the different systems. This is mainly how the virus spreads and why it's so successful; it entices victims to click on the mailed attachments because they're usually from people they know and trust. The virus, however, only works with Outlook, not Outlook Express.

The virus does not destroy files and other resources, but it can disable corporate and other mail servers. On the same day the virus was released, March 26th, 1999, the Microsoft Corporation shut down all incoming emails. Other companies such as Intel also reported being affected by the virus.

Some people also found a twist in the virus. A small percentage of cases reported that when the day of the month is the same as the minute value, the current cursor position carries a payload of text, pulled from the word game Scrabble and a Bart Simpson cartoon. Payload, in hacking terms, pertains to the part of the malware, mostly viruses, that executes the malicious activity.

At the end of the day, the United States' department for computer emergencies along with several anti-virus software sites, warned the pubic of the virus and then developed an antivirus to counter it.

So, how does a user avoid the Melissa virus? Knowing that the virus exists and spreads through emails and attachments doesn't ultimately mean that you need to stop using and reading your emails. You simply need to learn how to screen the messages you receive and be wary of the attachments that you choose to open. If or when you receive an email that contained the subject line and body text as mentioned previously, know better than to open the attachment. Simply copy the email address of the person the email came from and let them know that their computer has been infected. You can delete the email as soon as you're done copying the sender's email address.

While on the topic of viruses, one virus called Stuxnet receives both praise and fear from all who know it. It is widely known by any hacker in the world, both amateurs and veterans. It's coined the virus that could have ignited World War III. In June of 2010, the malicious computer worm Stuxnet was found in the data banks of power plants, traffic control systems, and factories around the world. It's not the first virus to target industrial control systems, but it's the first malware that had the ability to spy on and undermine the industrial control systems. It had the ability to turn up the pressure inside nuclear reactors or switch off oil pipelines. All the while telling the system operators that everything was functioning normally.

Stuxnet at the time was 20 times more complex than any other virus code. It didn't carry the usual forged security clearance that most viruses had to tunnel into systems, instead it had actual clearance – stolen from reputable technology companies all over the world.

The virus took advantage of zero days – security gaps that the systems creators were unaware of. Most of the most successful viruses exploit these security gaps, many of which can be found on the black market priced at over $100,000. Stuxnet, however, had and took advantage of 20 zero days.

Unlike most malware, Stuxnet didn't always activate and harm all the computers, networks, and systems it infects. Deep into the Stuxnet code was specific configuration requirements, in short, it had a target. Without the target, the virus would remain dormant. It was a marksman's job. When the virus finds its target, it fakes industrial process control sensor signals. These signals tell the infected system that there's nothing wrong, allowing the virus to control the system without letting it shut down because of the abnormal behaviour.

While the virus was found in many countries including Pakistan, the United States, Indonesia, and India, the main affected country was Iran, with almost 60% of their computers and systems infected. Stuxnet was looking to shut down the centrifuges that spin nuclear material at Iran's enrichment facilities, which could lead to mass destruction.

This was the point where Stuxnet stopped being a complex malware and became an actual weapon. The first one to be made completely out of a code.

The virus may have shut down a thousand centrifuges at Natanz, Iran's main enrichment facility, by forcing a change in the centrifuge's rotor speed. The virus would raise the speed and then slow it down, consequently creating excessive vibrations or distortions that would destroy the centrifuge.

In November 2010, the International Atomic Energy Agency, the agency that maintained surveillance over nuclear activities for the United Nations, reported that Iran has suspended work at its nuclear facilities without stating a clear reason why. This led people to credit Stuxnet.

In the following months, the Iranian government conceded that the Bashir nuclear facility, which at that time was still under construction, was infected by the virus. This meant that switching on the power plant could lead to a national electricity blackout.

In response to this cyberattack, Iran issued an open call for hackers to join the Iranian Revolutionary Guard – the second largest online army in the world.

Up to this day no creator nor country has admitted responsibility for the creation of the famous virus. There are speculations, however, that it was a jointly built American/Israeli cyberweapon. The virus code apparently referenced several Hebrew Bible terms and verses, connecting it to Israel. Many also believe that the United States was involved because it's the leading country in technological advancement – powerful and knowledgeable enough to craft one of the most complex malware to ever exist. Some have also speculated the involvement of *Siemens*, a mobile phone company whose software is used by the Iranian regime.

The same mobile company, however, was responsible for the detection and removal tool for Stuxnet. Kn the first few months of the virus' discovery, Siemens successfully developed a removal tool that eradicated the virus in computers. On its first run, over 20 customers' systems were successfully free of the virus, and the tool didn't have any other damaging effects, unlike other companies' attempts.

The discovery of a 100% successful removal tool launched after a few months, but the creator of the Stuxnet itself remained unknown.

The most important question might not be who designed it, but who will *redesign* it?

Months after the detection of Stuxnet, it became available online for anyone to download and tinker with. Stuxnet was the first ever virus that had the potential to crash power grids, destroy oil pipelines, and ultimately cause a nationwide panic. What makes it scarier than it already is, is that it's an open-source weapon. Anyone can play with it, pull it apart, and create new ways to put the virus to use.

These are only five of the famous cases known around the cybercrime world. There are countless others, some considered less notorious, some quite possibly bordering on insane. And although most of them spread fear, one cannot help but marvel at these cybercrimes. Just like any other crime, for it to succeed, ample planning, the right strategy, and in the case of cybercrimes, the right code or equipment are all needed. Just because the crimes begun to stray off of the streets and required less physical contact and leg work, doesn't mean its effects on its victims are also down to a minimum. These famous cases and several others are proof of just how frightening cybercrime actually is. People behind their laptops can hack into a system, a network, or a computer from the other side of the globe. They can even rob banks without ever needing to put a mask on. They can terrorize without having to hold a gun. And they can create weapons of terror without gunpowder. So, how do they do it? *Where* do they do it?

Chapter 2: The Dark Web

The Dark Web exists on darknets and is a small part of the deep web – the part of the World Wide Web that is impossible to be indexed and found by search engines. This is where most cybercrimes are plotted, and a place where most hacker lurk around. The darknets that constitute the dark web are networks run either by public organizations or individuals. These networks can be peer-to-peer but can also be large networks such as the famous Tor.

The Onion Router, or more commonly known as Tor, is one of the first encrypted networks. It's widely known among hackers and lurkers of the dark web because it has become an avenue for cybercrime — especially, drug trafficking. And what's ironic about it is that it was invented by the United States government. The popular network allows for online anonymity using a method called Onion Routing. Instead of your computer directly connecting to a website when you go online, it passes through different encryptions before going through an exit node that finally connects you to the website you want to visit. The Onion Router was created in 1995, at the US Naval Research Lab. Paul Syverson, one of the co-creators of Tor, explained how they came to create the popular network: they thought about how intelligence agents, or what common folk regard as spies, could do to protect their identities online. The normal side of the internet, the one you're most likely using right now, can be easily manipulated and altered if someone knows what he's doing. Conversations can be tracked, calls tapped, and identities revealed. When your computer directly connects to a website, these are made even easier. So, Paul Syverson and his team at the Naval Research Lab made a network that disabled all of these. Thus, the creation of one of the most widely used networks on the dark web.

While it's primary purpose was far from becoming an avenue for crime to be plotted and committed, many have seen and utilized the convenience of the dark web and the anonymity it offers.

The dark web is a powerful tool that stops others — everyone — from tracking online activities. And while it provides secure communications between person to person, especially for sensitive topics that require conversations that cannot be hacked into, it also provides hackers with a place to communicate and conduct illegal activities without being tracked by anyone, especially law enforcement.

Since its creation, the dark web has also served as a black market for hackers, both the amateurs and the veterans. It's the best place to sell everything illegal; credit card information, malware codes for famous viruses that people can tinker with, and illegal substances to name a few. Transactions are often done through digital currencies such as bitcoin. This allows for anonymous transactions, which, as you can probably tell, is crucial for these types of businesses. Things for sale on the dark web can cost up to as much as $100,000 and possibly even more. The return in the investment, however, is a great promise. The Silk Road is probably one of the most recognized black market in the dark web, but we won't discuss that in this section. We'll get to that.

While the anonymity that the dark web offers is undoubtedly a contributory factor to the success of cybercrime, people must keep in mind that it is merely the tool used in cybercrime.

Chapter 3: Kali Linux and Its Tools

It all seems easy when you read it in print. A hacker *hacks*, earns money from his cybercrimes, and then tries his best to not be caught by the law. Hacking, however, isn't as simple as a hacker snapping his fingers and a virus code or a special malware magically appears. Hacking requires *actual* work, several resources, and a knack for coding. So where do hackers begin?

The answer may be Kali Linux. It is a Linux distribution designed for digital forensics and penetration testing. Nearly every professional hacker uses Linux or Unix as their operating systems. Aside from a few hacking tools, most are developed for Linux, which is why, as a beginning hacker, one must know how to work with from a Linux distribution — such as Kali Linux — and have at least the basic Linux skills.

Kali Linux has several security tools in its arsenal. A few of the most commonly used and well-known are Aircrack-ng, Burp suite, Ettercap, John the Ripper, Kismet, and Wireshark. The tools can be categorized through their main functions: Vulnerability Analysis, Information Gathering, We Applications, Wireless Attacks, Exploitation Tools, Stress Thinking, Forensics Tools, Password Attacks, Sniffing and Spoofing, Reverse Engineering, Maintaining Access, Hardware Hacking, and Reporting Tools,.

Kali Linux also offers metapackages that can be customized depending on what the user might need it for. The subsets of tools in each metapackage vary. For example, a customized Kali ISO is for security assessments that are wireless. A user can customize this metapackage even more by including other wireless tools subsets.

To be an expert at the craft of hacking, veteran hackers believe that one should master a few Linux skills and work from a Linux distribution such as Kali Linux.

Linux basics such as configuring apache, using startup scripts, managing hard drives. There are also more advanced tutorials such as performing general reconnaissance for successful cybercrime attacks and intercepting and decrypting Windows passwords.

There are several tutorials on how Linux works, specifically Kali, but the most important learning experience is to try it out on your own and have a go at it.

Chapter 4: Website Hacking

The most basic things most people know about hackers, aside from the fact that they hack into accounts, is that they can hack into websites. As the security of websites gets tighter and tighter, hackers also become ever more sophisticated with their hacking methods. Hackers have also built online communities where people can work together and share their own secrets of the trade. Discoveries of new web application intrusions and malicious software codes are posted in forums by these close-knit community of hackers. These web application intrusions are almost always updated.

With most businesses conducting their sales on the internet and popular websites that gain a significant amount of traffic, it's a no brainer why websites are targets for hackers. The internet provides web-based technologies that make conducting businesses easier; there are web applications that allows easier communication between suppliers, dealers, and customers, and transactions are made easier through online payments. These web-based technologies, however, have also opened up vulnerabilities in businesses. Previously unknown security risks can know become backdoors for hackers to infiltrate a business' website and conduct a cyber crime attack.

There are several reasons why hackers choose to hack websites and in this section, we're going to look at a few of the most common.

A common reason is to hack a website for sensitive data. Websites store valuable information such as credit card numbers and login details. Especially in businesses, websites most likely ask customers for information using submission forms and login pages. When a website is hacked, hackers can have all the access to this information. When they get their hands on sensitive information such as those regarding identities, and credit card numbers, for instance, businesses can be done for.

When hackers breach through the security of company or business owned websites, this causes a substantial reputational damage. Clients will no longer trust the company or business and will most likely opt for another organization, and quite rightfully so.

Another reason hackers have for hacking into websites is to launch phishing sites. Phishing is further discussed in its own section in this book. But to give you a general idea, hackers can input malicious code in vulnerable web applications within websites, this malicious software can then trick users and redirect them to a phishing site where they may be fooled into giving up sensitive information, under the belief that they're still on a safe site. This kind of attack can be achieved through various hacking methods, and one is called an SQL Injection. SQL stands for *Structured Query Language* and an SQL Injection is an injection attack that utilizes any website or web application that uses an SQL-based database. Attackers can execute malicious payload that allows them to control a web application's database server.

What makes this scary is that it can attack websites even when owners may think that they are secure. An SQL Injection vulnerability remains to be one of the oldest, most prevalent and most dangerous of web application vulnerabilities.

On a Phishing-related note, website hacking can also lead to hackers sharing illegal content on hacked websites. Illegal content may include child sexual abuse, child pornography, and content instructing or promoting crime or violence. A hacker can distribute these through hacked websites so when law enforcement finds the website, the hacker isn't the one who's going to be charged, but the innocent and unknowing website owner.

Another reason why hackers are hacking websites is to abuse bandwidth. Bandwidth is the maximum amount of data that can be transmitted in a certain amount of time. It's usually measured through bits per second or bps, and the larger the bandwidth, the more expensive it is. Illicit activities may need larger bandwidth so that they can transmit more data - such as pirated software - faster and more efficiently. Hackers can hack into a victim's server with a big bandwidth and use it without the victim even knowing.

Other hack attempts, however, are merely designed for SEO purposes - to boost a website's rankings on Google. Hackers can inject hidden keywords on different sites. When this happens to websites run by businesses, it could have serious repercussions. One, because search engines do not allow this activity and they can give the hacked website penalties. And two, because this can put the business' website to the risk of being eliminated from the search engine's listing.

There are several resources such as tutorials on how to hack websites, there are even online courses on them. And the reason why they aren't taken down or considered illegal is that these skills can actually be used by budding web developers, system administrators, and computer programmers. By understanding *how* website hacking happens, then can learn how to counter it and build better security. There's a thing called "Ethical Hacking", where people can practice hacking for ethical and legal purposes. Sites such as Hack This Site! on hackthissite.org is a legal and safe network security resource where users can test their hacking skills and interact with other hackers in forums and online discussion boards.

So, how are website hackings attacks prevented?

Sophisticated hacker attacks like the previously mentioned SQL Injection and Cross Site Scripting can be difficult to arm websites for, but it's not impossible. The first step to preventing these sophisticated attacks is to establish which of your web applications have vulnerabilities, if there are any at all. The best way to accomplish this to launch your own attacks on your web applications and see if they work. Another way to protect your website against attacks like these and any other hacker methods is through tools that do the security work for you. There are several products in the market, and they're a good investment, especially for businesses. Most of these tools, applications, and products can ensure web application security as well as identifying vulnerabilities, if any, exist in your web applications.

Chapter 5: Server Hacking

A web server, also known as an internet server, is a computer system that stores files such as web pages and then delivers these content and services to users through the internet or a network. Web servers are basically the systems that host websites, web applications, and web services, and makes them accessible via the internet. Web servers do this by returning HTML files over an HTTP connection – the most basic protocol when giving out information in the internet. So, a web server basically responds to HTTP requests to bring content to a user.

You can imagine a web server as a part of a stack. Something like Jenga blocks. The bottom most layer is a network, next is an operating system, and then applications, a database, and then finally the web server where third-party applications and custom web applications are stacked on top of. And just like with Jenga, if the bottom layers are compromised, the web server and everything above it on the tier can be compromised.

As we've mentioned in the previous section, most organizations have websites. Nowadays, customers turn to these websites for convenient buying and selling of products and services. So, websites store valuable information such as credit card numbers, email addresses and passwords, etc. This fact alone has made websites targets to attackers. To reach a website, however, a hacker must go through a web server first.

In this section of the book, we will discuss everything that has to do with web servers and what it takes to hack into them. We'll look at the different types of web servers, the different vulnerabilities that hackers can exploit in web servers as well as the type of attacks they can launch on these vulnerabilities and the tools they use to launch these attacks, and finally, how to avoid attacks on web servers.

Let's take a look at what makes up a web server first. A web server requires both hardware and software. So, it has a physical server, a server operating system, and the software that's used to facilitate the HTTP communication and requests. So, the term "web server" can refer to the hardware or web server software.

There are hundreds of servers that currently exist, but two of the most popular systems are Apache and Microsoft's IIS. Below is a list of the most common we servers that people on the internet use to host their websites.

Microsoft's Internet Information Services (IIS) – A web server developed by Microsoft, intended for the use of the Windows NT family. Needless to say, it runs on Windows. It hosts most asp and aspx websites and is the second most used web server on the internet. According to Netcraft, an internet services company based in Bath, England, IIS had a market share of 32.80% on all existing websites - falling behind Apache, which had 38.22%.

Apache – Apache, formally called Apache HTTP Server, is under an open community of developers of the Apache Software. They developed this free and open-source cross-platform web server to host most PHP websites. While it's cross platform, it's usually installed on Linux. It is the most commonly used web server on the internet.

Apache Tomcat – Apache Tomcat or simply the Tomcat server, is an open-source web container also developed by Apache Software Foundation. And because it interacts with Java servlets, most Java server pages or JSP websites are hosted in Apache Tomcat servers.

There are countless others web servers including Google's own in-house developed software stack, the GWS, and a web server that can also be used as a reverse proxy called Nginx, to name a few of other web servers.

Just like websites, web servers also have vulnerabilities. Hackers and attackers alike exploit these vulnerabilities to gain unauthorized entry to the server, and thus control of the websites it hosts.

One of the most common vulnerabilities is the default setting of web servers. These default settings such as the default user IDs and passwords can easily be cracked by attackers by merely guessing. Default settings also allow running commands on the server which can be exploited by hackers.

Another vulnerability is the misconfiguration of operating systems and networks. Different operating systems and networks can have different configurations, which are controlled by the user. Most, if not all, configurations allow the user to run commands on the server. If the user doesn't have a strong password, these configurations could land in the wrong hands and be potentially dangerous.

As with anything related to technology these days, operating systems and web servers can also have bugs and glitches on them. These bugs, when discovered by hackers, can also be exploited to gain access to the servers. This will ultimately give the hackers unauthorized access to anything that the web server hosts.

And of course, the most common vulnerability with every device, system, and network: the lack of proper security. Needless to say, lax security creates loopholes for hackers and attackers alike. Users should always make sure that they have a running antivirus and that it's up to date. Their operating systems and web server software should also have the latest patches.

Now that we know the common vulnerabilities of web servers that can be exploited, let's take a look at the types of attacks hackers can launch on them, as well as the reasons why hackers launch them. What do successful web server hacking attacks offer and what effect do they have?

The first type is called a Denial of Service or DOS attack. Hackers basically overload a web server by sending multiple service request packets. This slows down the web server, ultimately causing programming errors that can then be exploited by the hackers.

As previously mentioned, web servers can have bugs. The type of attacks that exploits these bugs to gain access to the web servers and execute operating system commands is called a Directory Traversal attack. This type of attack allows hackers to access sensitive information about the user, install malicious software on the user's computers, or gain unauthorized entry to restricted directories. A similar attack called Sniffing not also exploits bugs, but also unprotected data sent over the network. These data may be intercepted, and with the correct methods, can lead to unauthorized access to the web server that the data is being sent to.

Another type of attack that's more like website hacking is domain hijacking. This is further discussed in its own section in the latter parts of the book, but it basically means that the Domain Name System or DNS settings are changed so that when users visit the website or domain name registered on a server, they are redirected to another site that can be fraudulent. The traffic that the original domain has will also be redirected to the fake sit. These fake sites can ask the user for sensitive information such as login information, credit card numbers, and passwords. Users may be tricked into inputting these pieces of information under the impression that they're on the real site. Hackers can then use the information they collected to commit more cybercrimes such as identity theft, money laundering, and credit card theft and fraud.

Compromised web servers can also be used to set-up websites that contain malicious software. When a user is redirected to the fake website, viruses and Trojans can be downloaded onto the user's computer.

If an attack like this is successfully launched on a big company's website, the company may face lawsuits from their clients, business losses, and reputational damage.

Speaking of reputational damage, aside from using the hijacked domain or website to redirect users to a fraudulent site, hacking a web server can also lead to defacement. This is most applicable to organizations or companies with big names and a reputation to protect. Hackers can take control of the web servers, which also gives them access to websites. They can change the content of the website into web pages that can cause reputational damage, such as, say, turning a respectable website into a pornography website. This type of attack is also used when hackers want to "expose" a certain company or organization.

Other types of attacks include phishing, which was previously mentioned in the Website Hacking section and further discussed on its own section, pharming, and SQL injection attacks.

To execute these different types of attacks on web servers, hackers have an arsenal of hacking tools. Here we list down some of the tools of the trade. They are used by hackers and even security professionals.

> Metasploit – This tool is often found as one of the first things people have on their list of tools used in hacking. It's basically the most standard hacking tool people use, mainly because it allows even the most beginner level hacker to run complex commands for specific attacks. It's generally used to create payloads – which as we've mentioned previously, is the component of a malware that causes the damage and does the dirty work. Metasploit is also very flexible: it's a framework that supports most, if not all, the popular operating systems, and can hack web applications, operating systems, and of course, web servers.

> Wireshark – Another household name not only to hackers, but also to security administrators. Wireshark is a protocol analyzer, meaning it allows the user to both capture and analyse both data and data traffic through virtually any network source, such as Wi-Fi networks or satellite links. This tool is so widely used because of the types of data it can capture: basically, any file format available and used on the internet. And just like Metasploit, Wireshark is compatible with all the popular operating systems. This tool is utilized in web server attacks such as Sniffing.

> Network Mapper or Nmap – This tool is used in, as the name suggests, network discovery, as well as security auditing. Nmap, in the most general sense, maps a network and identifies information about a network such as what hosts, services, and operating systems are being used. This tool is often used to combat certain anti-hacking security tools

deployed by users. Nmap is also part of a popular security suite that contains other common tools such as Zenmap, Ncat, and Nping. All of which have different functions from scanning graphical user interface to generating network packets.

MPack – This tool is a Russian developed PHP-based malware kit. Unlike the previously mentioned tools, MPack is solely a web exploitation tool that's used to hack a web server and redirect all traffic from a safe and legitimate site to fraudulent sites, which are mostly websites that contain malicious software.

SQLMap – Remember the SQL or *Structured Query Language* injections that were mentioned earlier? Tools like SQLMap makes the process of detecting SQL injections easier. It does, however, also make SQL injection attacks stronger because it can detect flaws in SQL injections and help a hacker make these flaws work for them, thus creating a stronger SQL injection. SQLMap is considered one of the ultimate penetration testers.

Zeus – Often called ZeuS or Zbot, Zeus isn't exactly a tool, but a type of malware. It's not just a malware though. It's the largest botnet on the internet. Botnets will be mentioned again throughout this book, but it's basically internet-connected devices that are running bots. This malware can steal data through several methods such as form grabbing. It's difficult to spot and spreads fast through downloads.

So, not that we know the types of attacks and some of the tools used to execute them, as well as what successful server hacking attacks can do, we can now start finding out how to protect ourselves from these attacks.

There are several policies and precautions that both organizations and individuals can implement to protect their web servers from exploitation. Listed below are some of the countermeasures to avoid attacks on web servers.

Proper patch management. This means a user should always make sure that their web servers are updated and installed with patches that help secure the web server. Patches are updates that addresses problems that arise with the software. Regular patch updates should be monitored and installed.

Avoid using default configuration. As mentioned in the vulnerabilities, configurations allow the user to run commands on the server. Misconfigurations of operating systems and software can lead to web servers being easier to hack into.

With that said, users must keep configuration files safe and secure. The configuration of the operating system as well as the web server software must be secure.

Invest in a good vulnerability scanning system. Web servers, as we've discussed, has a *lot* of vulnerabilities. Having a tool that scans for vulnerabilities, so a user can address them before hacker exploits them is a good countermeasure against web server hacking.

Use Firewalls with updated signatures. Firewalls blocks traffic that is coming from unidentified IP addresses, which could be the IP address of an attacker.

Have an anti-virus installed and have it updated regularly. The use of an anti-virus program is highlighted to every user time and time again. They don't exist for no reason, they help users build layers of protection on their systems, computers, and networks. And they can stamp out any malware present on your server.

Block unnecessary protocols. Some services may be merely bloatware — web applications that aren't really used anymore. These should be blocked to avoid being exploited by hackers.

In the same sense, default accounts as well as unused accounts should be removed and deleted. Then follow a strict access control policy for the system.

Disable remote administration.

Make sure the operating systems and software used in web servers are properly installed, up to date, and secured by anti-virus programs.

Chapter 6: Social Engineering Tools

Appeal to authority, emotion, and greed: these are the common techniques used in an array of malicious activities called Social Engineering. These malicious activities are accomplished mainly through human interactions, thus the name *social* engineering. Most Social Engineering attacks rely simply on the victim's willingness to help. Hackers may pose as a friend, family, or co-worker of a victim, simply asking for a little bit of help such as access to additional network resources.

Social Engineering usually happens through a series of steps, which begin with the attacker gathering information about their victim. Vital information may include their victim's background, family, company – all of which can be possible points of entry. The attacker then uses these pieces of information to gain the victims trust and fool them into giving up sensitive information.

Social Engineering is also mentioned in the Phishing section of this book as it's a vital part of gathering information from victims for phishing attacks. Aside from its uses in Phishing Attacks, Social Engineering has several types. The most common include:

Baiting - Just as the actual definition of the word, baiting basically involves hackers or attackers luring people to either install malicious software on their computers or share sensitive information. The unique thing about baiting is that it doesn't need to make use of enticing offers like malvertising or fraudulent websites such as those involved in phishing attacks. Baiting makes use of a physical device, such as a USB flash drive or a hard drive. Attackers would place the device in a place where it's almost always sure to be picked up. Most of the time attackers put enticing labels on the devices to pique people's interest, and more often, their greed. The labels could say that it's a company's payroll list. When left in a public place such as a bathroom, parking lots, or even elevators, it's sure to be picked up by a greedy victim. What awaits him when he loads the device onto his computer, however, is an instant installation of malicious software in his system. These malware-infested devices are central to Baiting attacks. While it utilizes physical devices in attacks, baiting scams can also involve the aforementioned tactics in other cyber crimes like phishing and malvertising. Baiting attacks don't *need* to use fake sites or false but enticing advertisements, but it *can* use these along with the malware-infested physical device attacks to garner more victims and information that can be used in further social engineering attacks.

Scareware - Scareware, also called deception software, fraudware, or rogue scanner software, involves fooling targeted users into thinking that they're computers, systems, or networks are infected with malware. The attackers then prompts the targeted users to download software that will "remove" the malware that is infecting their computers, systems, or networks. But the catch is that the "solution" that the attackers offer are actually the software that may contain viruses, worms, and all other kinds of cyber filth. The most common example of scareware technique is the text boxes that pop-up in some websites, informing the user that their computer might be infected with malicious software. If this effectively scares the targeted users, they're bound to follow the "solution" that the attackers would offer, either a downloadable software or the targeted users would be redirected to a site that will download the "solution". The "solution" can be malware itself or a backdoor for attackers to gain unauthorized access on the victim's sensitive information. Another way that scareware works and spreads is through emails. Users may notice that sometimes they get spam emails offering false antivirus software that can clean their "infected" computers. These emails can also contain advertisements that look legit, but the software that they're advertising could be a fraudulent one that instead of keeping the user's computer secure, it installs malware and steals information.

Pretexting - Pretexting is a part of social engineering that lies a close to how identity theft works in the sense that the attackers or hackers are imposters. Attackers would pretend to be someone the targeted victim would trust such as relatives, friends, and family. They will ask the targeted victim for "crucial" information such as social security numbers and even financial details. Some attackers also pretend to be people of authority and will ask the targeted victim for what would seem like basic personal pieces of information such as name, date of birth, general location, and the like. Another way that attackers can gain these pieces of information is to pretend to be someone from a bank or pretend to be the targeted victim's financial manager. The imposter would then ask for the victim's name and all the other key information under the pretense that it will be used as verification for transactions. Attackers that launch pretexting scams will then use the information they gathered to craft clever webs of lies to obtain more sensitive information from their targets. Some go even as far as building an intimate friendship and then asking for a favor such as lending large amounts of money. Through pretexting scams, social engineers can gain all types of information from the victims.

Knowing the different types of social engineering attacks that can be launched against a user and knowing how to identify them is one of the defensive steps to make sure that you don't fall victim to these kinds of attacks. Security experts and those that are training to be security administrators actually practice penetrating systems using social engineering techniques. This will help them better understand how the attacks work and how to build better security against them. This type of training helps security experts and IT departments to assess how prepared their employees or fellow security administrators are when it comes to social engineering attacks.

As you can see, Social Engineering attacks rely heavily on evoking human emotions to be executed successfully. Social engineers make emails seem alarming, advertisements enticing, and their websites interesting. The moment a targeted user falls victim to these emotions, they also fall victim to social engineers' schemes at traps.

With this information, preventing becoming a victim to social engineers and their attacks can boil down to one major solution: users should always be alert. Social engineers do a lot of research in order to make their traps appealing, so users should always be wary. If it's too good to be true, it probably is.

Another good tip to improve a user's vigilance against social engineering attacks is to not open emails with suspicious attachments. Stay as far away as possible from sketchy sources and their downloadable content. Emails are common vectors for social engineering attacks so users should always be wary when opening emails — even if they're from the user's address lists. Just like the Melissa virus discussed in the Famous Cases section, some social engineered malware can pull out distribution lists from their victims' address books. Emails and email addresses can be easily faked, and some symbols swapped for the same looking ones so that they can fool users into thinking the emails are from a reliable source.

In relation to this, another tip is to be extra wary of tempting offers. Offers should also always be cross-checked and researched before accepting any. Search engines can easily show which offers are actually genuine. Users should always keep in mind that the offers created by social engineers are meant to look so good, no one can say no. That is, if they're not vigilant. The offers might be tempting, but users should keep in mind that they can also be a trap.

Another way users can protect themselves against social engineers is to increase the security of their accounts. Social engineers do a lot of research on their targeted victims and one of the most valuable pieces of information they can use against these targeted victims is the user's credentials. When social engineers get their hands on the targeted user's credentials, they can create more tempting offers and social engineering attacks that specifically cater to the targeted user. Utilizing multi-factor authentication can help ensure the safety of a user's accounts by not only requiring a mere password to gain access to an account. One of the easiest multi-factor authentication or 2FA to use is Imperva Incapsula Login protect.

As with all the cyber crimes in this book, the security tip that's mentioned time and time again is to have a solid antivirus software. Not only this, but users should always make sure that their security software are up to date and patched with the latest signatures. It's better if users have the software automatically updating regularly.

Chapter 7: Drug Trafficking

Now that we've covered some of the basics and two of the most common cyber crimes associated with hackers, website and server hacking, let's dig a little deeper. And just like in any operation, whether on the streets or on the internet, the more you dig deeper, the dirtier it all gets.

One of the biggest cybercrime stories in history involves an illegal drug trade or drug trafficking: the Silk Road – a black market for shrooms, marijuana, and MDMA. It's the prime example of drug trafficking, with 500 individual sellers and 25,000 unique items for sale, the Silk Road operation has earned a global revenue of over a billion dollars and has earned the title: eBay of Vice. The proprietor of the Silk Road has earned tens of millions of dollars through the commissions. He or she was unnamed and ultimately unknown until Chicago Homeland Security Investigations (HSI) agent Jared Der-Yeghiayan investigated Silk Road in June 2011.

On the 6th of February 2012, the proprietor introduced himself as Dread Pirate Roberts. A name taken from the 1987 fantasy film The Princess Bride. The name itself is a pseudonym used to instil fear – but the film later reveals that the owner of this name is actually a romantic man behind a mask. The internet is known to be a place where people can use aliases, pseudonyms, and alter egos – all for the freedom of expression. But also, for the possibility of actions without consequences.

On October 1st, 2013, a man named Ross Ulbricht was arrested for allegedly being the person behind Dread Pirate Roberts and the creator of the Silk Road. The marketplace was then taken down and the trial on Mr. Roberts ensued.

The big question, and something we can all learn from, is: how did the Silk Road last so long? It was literally a cornucopia of illegal goods – especially drugs. The Silk Road was a billion-dollar empire that churned money through bitcoins only using a laptop and a Wi-Fi connection. So, what took the FBI so long to track it down and take it down?

The Silk Road wasn't on the regular internet – not the one most people know and use. It was released on what is colloquially called the Dark Web or the Dark Net. As discussed earlier in the book, the dark web allows people to stop others from tracking their online activities. The dark web also protects people's identities and allows for complete anonymity – a powerful tool in drug trafficking.

Another reason is that the Silk Road traded exclusively in a cryptocurrency called Bitcoin. Bitcoin was invented by "Satoshi Nakamoto" in 2008. It was the first decentralized digital currency or what is now more commonly known as cryptocurrency. This type of digital currency didn't need banks for transactions, money can be sent directly from person to person. There was no central authority that oversaw transactions, and everyone involved in the cryptocurrency had their own encrypted digital wallets.

The combination of the dark web and Bitcoin give people — especially Dread Pirate Roberts, the owner of Silk Road — a sense of security.

However, an overly exaggerated sense of security isn't a good thing. An operation called Marco Polo shut down the Silk Road and arrested Ross Ulbricht, along with 14 other people. The FBI had been watching the Silk Road operations for a period of time, waiting for Dread Pirate Roberts or Ross Ulbricht to make a small slip – and he made several. From the FBI connecting his fake ID's to screenshots of his laptop showing that he was allegedly on the admin page of Silk Road and was operating an avatar with a name Dread Pirate Roberts. Ross Ulbricht was convicted of eight charges including money laundering, computer hacking, conspiracy to traffic narcotics, and attempting the murder of six people. He is serving a lifetime in prison without the possibility of parole.

On 6 November 2013, however, Silk Road 2.0 came online, run by former administrators of Silk Road. But it was shortly shut down a year later and the operator was arrested.

From this viewpoint, online drug trafficking is prominently viewed as something that the Feds will immediately shut down the moment they find out about it, but several people have spoken up on how this it's not as bad as it seems. These people argue that it could be an accepted alternative that's more peaceful than both the global and local drug wars that almost always involves violence and the death of innocent people. Several proponents and sites similar to the Silk Road also attest that buying narcotics from the safety of their homes is better than acquiring it from people – mostly criminals – on the street.

As you can probably tell, hackers play a central and essential role in online drug trafficking. Expert money launderers and drug traffickers collaborate with hackers – the specialists in system penetration, network exploration, or data extraction. It doesn't help that dark web, the underground part of the internet, can deliver industrial grade products anonymously, while also offering hackers illegal control over machinery without proper credentials. All of which are ingredients to the perfect drug trafficking scheme.

Chapter 8: Illegal Content

It's merely the beginning of this book, but you have probably already guessed that existing cyber crimes aren't just website and serving hacking and drug trafficking. The internet has opened up an array of different cyber crimes and illegal activities on the internet. These illegal activities can be categorized into two branches:

1. Illegal activity or cyber crimes that can be investigated and prosecuted by the Law Enforcement.
2. Civil illegal activities that can be both investigated and prosecuted by a wide range of civilian bodies such as INHOPE.

INHOPE consists of the INHOPE Association and the INHOPE Foundation. INHOPE is an International Association of Internet Hotlines. They are an active and collaborative global network of Hotlines whose mission is to stamp out the cybercrime that we will discuss in this section: the distribution of illegal content over the internet.

INHOPE focuses on eliminating child sexual abuse from the Internet, but they also deal with generally illegal content found on the internet. INHOPE encourages people to help them in their mission to eradicate the internet of illegal content, advising people to report anything that is suspected to be a child sexual abuse image or video. Through the group's industry and law enforcement partners, they take down any content that is illegal.

To fully understand this, we need to know what actually constitutes as illegal content on the internet. This section will highlight the different types of illegal content commonly found around the web.

In 2011, 18 million child pornography files are reported. Since 2007, no less than 5 million are reported annually. And the numbers aren't exactly stagnant. These numbers are constantly growing. For some people it might be hard to imagine pornographic pictures and videos of children, and therefore do not understand what is meant by "child pornography". In several countries, this type of illegal content is called CASM or "child sexual abuse material". This is to reinforce that behind child pornography materials, there is sexual abuse of real children.

It's an ongoing challenge to define what constitutes child pornography because different countries also have different legal definitions. The broadest and most common definition of child pornography is any form of media that depicts the involvement, often forced participation, and engagement of children in explicit sexual activities.

There are, however, several factors that come into play with this definition. Different countries have different ages of consent, so child sexual abuse material laws in one country might not apply to another. This, along with disagreements on what actually constitutes as child pornography and if the possession of it is a crime, makes it more difficult for organizations to completely stamp out the stream of these kinds of illegal content lurking in the internet. Organizations, however, encourage that anything users might suspect as illegal content should be reported.

Content like child pornography are often shared through websites, most of which aren't for commercial purposes. Often, they're just for self-gratification and as a service to people who "like" the same thing. However, with the rise of digital currencies and the ability to direct payments without the compromise of identity, child pornography websites are transitioning into commercial websites themselves - charging people a fee for access to a plethora of illegal content. This usually involves sites which are password protected. A user simply has to pay a subscription fee in order to get the password and open the website virtually anywhere in the world.

The difference in what counts as legal in different countries gives illegal content creators and distributors a loophole to work with. Most sites with illegal content are hosted in places where there are no legal regulations regarding the distribution of these illegal content.

Websites, however, aren't the only way to distribute illegal content like child pornography. Peer-to-Peer File Sharing Networks are also vectors that can help illegal content creators to distribute their materials with a minimal fee.

The production of illegal content such as child pornography on the internet has given rise to groups called "Pedophile Rings". They are comprised of several people who share the same goal: to create and distribute child sexual abuse material without being caught. Members of these groups are usually scattered all over the world, in different legal jurisdictions. They all share experiences and tips on how to avoid detection by the law enforcement and organizations such as INHOPE.

Pedophile rings also participate in another type of illegal activity that ultimately leads to the creation of illegal content. "Online Grooming" is a practice that involves pedophiles befriending a child, building their trust and creating an emotional connection in order to push a hidden agenda such as sexual abuse and exploitation, as well as trafficking. Children can be "groomed" through face-to-face interactions, but social media platforms, online forums, and online communication applications such as Skype, are often used by pedophiles and traffickers because they offer easy access to private one-on-one conversations with their victims.

Pedophiles will often act as children themselves in online forums or social media platforms to gain the targeted child's trust. Most young people would assume that places on the internet such as discussion boards are public, so they shouldn't be worried, but pedophiles and online human traffickers are getting more and more sophisticated with their methods. Sometimes when they've established a level of trust with their victims, they would actually start sending samples of sexual activity content, such as pornographic images. This allows pedophiles and human traffickers to gauge the reaction of their child victim and whether they would be "willing" participants.

While blocking a user's access to sites that create and distribute illegal content can save the user from seeing the horrors of these content, it isn't the solution to eradicating the internet of these illegal content creators and distributors. The best way is still to report any suspicious websites that might be spreading illegal content. When users practice zero tolerance for child sexual abuse content on the internet, they help the law and organizations to stamp out illegal content. It's the small steps that help perpetuate a big change.

Chapter 9: Fake News

Over a decade ago, "Fake News" wasn't in people's screens, much less on newsstands and newspapers themselves. In fact, it was barely in the vocabularies of people. Nowadays, however, it's a term that is used so often that it has become 2017's word of the year. This would seem like a harmless fact, but fake news is seen as one of the greatest threat to the threads of society.

The emergence of the Internet in the 90s provided everyone easy access to information, whether that information was true or false didn't matter. Through time the internet has grown to unbelievable proportions, and so has the amount of information that it contained and gave access people to. Information on the internet can come from anyone — meaning anyone can be a perpetrator of fake news.

Fake news is a contributing branch of yellow journalism and yellow press — these are news outlets and newspapers with "news" that have little to no research backing the truths to it. It uses eye-catching and often fabricated headlines for sales, instead of reporting actual facts for the sake of imparting knowledge. Articles, videos, and any other form of media that's intended to entice people using mere titles and offer useless or unrelated content is often called "click bait". Click baits increase the financial profit and following of the websites that they're in. These and other types of fake news rely highly on editorial bias and exaggerations of news events. It also utilizes appealing to the emotions of the reader while intentionally omitting facts from things that might have happened in real life.

The relevance of fake news has increased in post-truth politics. Aside from the sales, another reason why people spread fake news is to mislead readers, especially when it comes to socio-political issues. There are "government actors" that propagate fake news, especially during elections. Fraudulent news websites constantly churn out content with fabricated headlines and exaggerated events.

Jestin Coler was the former founder and CEO of *Disinfomedia*, a company that owned many faux news websites. He has jump started a business out of producing fake news that was published in several fraudulent sites. He has shared that he had 20 t0 25 writers working for him. His company and his people were responsible for several fake news articles, one of which got 1.6 million views in only 10 days. The headline that got *that* much traffic was about an FBI agent that was found dead in his apartment. What made it even more interesting was that this agent was connected to the Hillary Clinton email issue.

Jestin Coler said that he was stunned at how fast news spread, even if it was fake. He was also taken aback by how fast people accepted and believed the fake news as well. Fake news took off especially during the election period in the United States. He said that anybody with a blog could simply write fake news about Trump and get a big number of followers.

Jestin Coler shared that the entire news article about the dead FBI Agent connected to Hillary Clinton email was fake. None of it was real; the town, the FBI agent, the people. He said people wanted to hear these kinds of stories, so he wrote them. And he earned money from it. Between $10,000 to $30,000 a month to put a figure to it.

But how did *Disinfomedia* earn money for writing fake news? The answer lies on the ads. Justin Coler said that the industry was a good place for targeting Trump supporters. With the large following that grew in fake news websites, companies and businesses were bound to put their ads on there.

Google, however, through its new policy, flags sites as fake news. When a site is flagged, Google would stop running ads on it. One of Justin Coler's sites were flagged — NationalReport.net — but there were lots of other ad networks that wanted to fill that advertisement space for fake news websites with lots of traffic.

Coler says that money gives fake news perpetrators a big push in publishing even more fake news. And while he is ready to leave the fake news business, he believes that there are many out there who will replace him. They know fake news pays and it's as easy as thinking of a story that will seem relevant. The internet is growing bigger by the day and it will continue to grow, each day becoming a bigger and bigger avenue for people to peddle more misinformation.

The spread of fake news everywhere on the internet has become a battle with the truth. Legitimate news stories now have to compete with fictional and made-to-entice headlines from fake news websites. It undermines serious media coverage and makes it difficult for serious journalists to cover stories. And because the internet gives everyone a mask and allows people to stay anonymous, fake news websites are becoming harder and harder to prosecute and charge with libel.

Fake news websites and articles currently flood the internet. It is becoming increasingly hard for people on the internet to discern which is fact and which is fiction. Hackers, scammers, fraudsters, and fake news writers alike often pose as legitimate news outlets but lack a known publisher.

Due to the prominence of fake news, social media platforms such as Facebook has announced a new tool to combat fake news. Google has also released a 'Fact Checker' feature for news and search results. With the help of fact-checking websites such as PolitiFact and Snopes, Google's algorithms check the news item or search result to bring the user the most informative and results. While these are all good solutions, it's still important that users themselves know how to recognize fake news from real ones.

While these tools help users in fact checking the information they get from the internet, it's not perfect. The best way to determine and stamp out fake news is still to think critically whenever we read something online. It's easy to believe a single source. But only takes a while to cross reference, fact check, and do some research. Attackers, hackers, cybercriminals, and even real people who are part of the yellow press - they all exploit people's ignorance.

Chapter 10: Cyber Stalking

Cyberstalking, from the word itself, is the use of the internet to stalk, harass, or threaten an individual. It's also known as Internet stalking, e-stalking, and online stalking. This cybercrime can be perpetrated through various forms of electronic communication such as social media platforms like Facebook and Twitter, as well as email services, chat rooms, instant messaging clients, online forums, and even text messages. Cyberstalking is usually paired with the traditional stalking offline. While there is no current unified legal approach, different governments all over the world are paying more and more attention to this criminal practice that's quickly finding its way to the norm.

Cyberstalking can be closely related to cyberbullying and cyber luring in that all three aims to harm a person without revealing their identities, thinking that just because they're behind a computer they are untouchable. Cyber stalkers highly rely on the anonymity provided by the internet. This allows them to send threats and harass a person without being detected.

Working to Halt Online Abuse or WHOA, an online organization dedicated to addressing online abuse, reported that cyber stalking began most often with emails, closely followed by online message boards and forum discussions, and then chat. Some cases of cyber stalking begin with traditional stalking incidents and then gets carried over to the internet. The opposite could also occur: stalking in the physical world could stem from cyber stalking. These types of stalking combined poses a threat to victims. In 1999, the murder of a woman from New Hampshire stemmed from cyber stalking. Her cyber stalker had sent her threats through emails and then posted on his website his plans on killing her.

Cyberstalking is different from spam in that it targets a certain individual, while spam casts a large net and targets a multitude of individuals by spamming messages.

A variation of cyber stalking is *Corporate Cyber Stalking* wherein an organization stalks a certain individual. This type of cyber stalking is usually utilized by people in high-ranking positions who have grudges on certain individuals — resulting in a power play. Corporate cyber stalking can also be done by any number of individuals in the same organization.

The internet has made it a lot easier for harassers to keep tabs on their victims through social media sites that allows the victims to share personal details seemingly without any consequences. Photos, videos, blog posts, and even current locations can be easily found in a person's profile pages on social media platforms. So, users must be careful on what they post online, one of the solutions to keep cyber stalkers away. If you don't give them any information to work with, they can never get to you. Stay anonymous just as the cyber stalkers are and keep your online presence to a minimum. Primary email addresses must be used for correspondence with caution as well. Email service providers can also help filter messages that a user receives — filtering all the unwanted spam.

Victims of cyber stalking are highly advised against meeting their stalkers in person, regardless of what they promise to give or not give. The most effective course of action to take if one ever finds himself having a cyber stalker, is to report the offender to other ISPs or internet service providers. Minors, who make up a surprisingly big percentage of cyber stalking victims, are advised to inform parents or a trusted adult as soon as they think they are being stalked. Attaining new email addresses and internet providers, as well as increasing security and privacy settings are all helpful in keeping cyber stalkers away. Law enforcement also advises victims to file complaints, log instances of harassment, and collect as much evidence as they can, without compromising their safety. The documentation can be used to explore legal avenues that the victim can take against the cyber stalker.

Chapter 11: Malware (Viruses, Spyware, and Bots)

The term "Malware", short for "malicious software", has been used throughout this book and in almost all the cybercrime cases mentioned, but what does it actually mean? It doesn't have one specific definition because malware is a general term for an array of cyber filth that's meant to damage a computer, a network, a system, or all of them. Back in the day, most malware were created by amateur teenagers who had nothing better to do - their malware simply infected computers and slowed them down or caused system damage. Nowadays, however, malware can be crafted by professional hackers and cybercriminals for cybercrimes such as cyber extortion and malvertising.

The most common example of malware is a computer virus. It's almost always attached to an executable file - meaning the virus won't infect the computer unless it's downloaded, installed, or manually run by a user. This is also the only way it can spread. It can exist on a system, but it won't spread until a user runs it. Viruses usually reach a user's computer through downloads from the internet. Files that a user downloads from the internet may have viruses on them, this is especially true in peer-to-peer file sharing and suspicious email attachments. So, why do hackers spread viruses? What do they do and how do they do it? Just like those previously mentioned viruses in the Famous Cases section, the Melissa virus and Stuxnet are viruses that are specially crafted for a specific purpose.

The Melissa virus hijacks a computer and puts the system's security down, while Stuxnet aims to control centrifuges and shut down power grids. Viruses can be coded to do an array of things, and a user only needs to click on it for it to spread.

However, viruses fall in only one of the many types under the malware umbrella. So, what are the other types?

Another type of malware is called a Trojan. Trojans are malware that look legitimate. They trick users into installing seemingly safe software on their computers. Trojans are especially dangerous because they can steal sensitive data, and at the same time allow cyber criminals access to these sensitive files and the user's system - creating what hackers call a backdoor. This is exactly what it's called. Trojans can give hackers unauthorized access to your computer once trojans infect it. And as you may have noticed in the trend of cybercrimes, the cyber criminals usually go after a user's financial information.

A similar type of malware that goes after a user's personal information is spyware. It's named exactly for what it does: spyware spies on a user's activities, lurking in the background and collecting or key logging sensitive information such as credit card numbers, login information, and user credentials.

A malware called Worms, on the other hand, doesn't need to spy on users or have to rely on a user manually downloading the malware. Worms self-replicate and spread through computer networks, causing major damage. They can infect computers through both local or internet accessed network interfaces. This type of malware easily spreads because it targets computers that are connected to other infected computers - they don't require hosts or even help from the user to spread and replicate. Computers that are infected by worms can cause security failures within systems and networks.

Another type of malware called ransomware or scareware is the most different among the mentioned types, but it's nonetheless sinister. Ransomware basically holds a user's computer hostage and asks for ransom to gain access again. They can threaten victims that their files will be deleted if the demanded amount is not met within a period of time. This is further discussed in its own section of this book. Adware is another type that relies on advertisements and is also further discussed in its different section under Malvertising.

Each of the different types of malware has their own way of working and spreading. While they all almost always target financial information, some of them, such as ransomware, focuses on getting money in a more direct way.

So, now that we know the different types of malware, what they do, and why they're spread by hackers, let's find out how to stop them.

The answer, as you will notice in several parts of this book, boils down to two things. First, is to gear up with protective tools. Antivirus software is one of the primary tools in combating malware. They are a good line of defense against cyber-attacks. Second, is the user's vigilance. Even if a computer is armed with a good up to date antivirus software, if a user carelessly opens email attachments, clicks hyperlinks, and downloads files from the internet, a computer can still be infected by malware. The easiest way to avoid getting infected by malware is to *avoid malware*. Users should always assume that things from the internet can be potentially harmful until actually proven to be safe. The saying prevention is better than cure holds true even for cybercrimes and cyber-attacks.

Chapter 12: Denial of Service

A Denial of Service attack or DoS attack happens when an attacker limits or completely takes away a user's access to computer systems, networks, devices, or other internet resources by shutting them down. This is accomplished by flooding targeted servers with traffic such as redundant requests. This causes the servers to overload and crash temporarily or fully shut down. Crashed servers are easily dealt with through a simple reboot of the system, but DoS attacks flood the servers, making it harder for servers to recover.

Denial of Service attacks have existed for quite a while, but as for its origins, some people speculate that it began with the attack delivered by the Morris worm, which is considered to be the very first computer worm that spread through the internet. Robert Tappan Morris, the namesake and creator of the worm, was a graduate student at Cornell University, and eventually became an assistant professor at Massachusetts Institute of Technology, were the computer systems that launched the worm was located. According to Robert Morris the worm was supposed to be a harmless intellectual exercise: to see just how big the internet is. Robert Morris was a computer scientist whose main interest of study was computer network architectures. Which is ironic because the supposedly unintended architecture of the code is what made it so dangerous. The spreading mechanism of the worm allowed computers to be infected by the worm over and over again, ultimately causing a Denial of Service attack. The Morris worm that he had created spread through the internet and caused buffer overflows that eventually led to successful DoS attacks on targeted systems.

Over 6,000 systems in the United States were affected by the worm and the damages that the worm caused were estimated at $100 million. Robert Morris was, however, prosecuted and received a 3-year probation sentence, along with a $10,000 restitution, and 400 community service hours.

Aside from its effects on the system and the ability to shut it down, the damage of Denial of Service attacks can also reach the hardware part of network resources. While causing successful buffer overflows can cause service interruptions, crippling physical structures and facilities such as the wirings can also count as Denial of Service attacks. This type of attack, however, can also be called sabotage. Attackers can damage physical structures by messing with a system's wiring, turning off cooling resources, and damaging a system's power source.

Hackers can basically target either the software or the hardware of systems or networks to launch a successful Denial of Service attack. So, how can users lessen the chances of falling victim to these attacks? The answer is to first determine if the system or network is already under a DoS attack. Determining if a system is undergoing a Denial of Service attack is the first step to saving a user's system from further physical infrastructure damages. So, how are systems under DoS attack determined? What are the signs?

First, a noticeable slowing on network performance – opening files on the network or accessing websites may be unusually slow. The inability to access certain websites as well as the inability or difficulty to access any site at all are also possible symptoms of an attack. When a system or network is under a DoS attack, a tell-tale sign is the increase in the number of spam emails that the user receives in their account.

However, users should also note that while these *could* mean that a system or a network is under a Denial of Service attack, not all disruptions in service and performance could immediately mean a DoS. These could merely be technical problems that can be fixed by the user's themselves or their network providers.

And if a user checks off all of these signs, then what? What does a user do if they think they're experiencing an attack?

If a user's computer is part of a larger network, which is the case in work computers, then the first things they need to do is to contact their network administrators. The unusual service degradation can be put to their attention and they can investigate further to see if the company's network is indeed under a Denial of Service attack.

However, if the user is using his home computer and he experiences all of the previously mentioned signs, then the next best thing is to contact their Internet Service Provider or ISP. The ISPs can usually tell the user if the network slowing down is a technical issue or an actual Denial of Service attack. In the case of a DoS attack, the ISP will advise the user on the appropriate course of action.

Chapter 13: Phishing

Fishing is the activity of trying to catch fish. A similar activity, also of a similar name, also carries the definition of an activity of trying to catch. The difference is that instead of fish, this activity tries to catch unknowing victims into giving sensitive information.

Phishing is a form of fraud that aims to gather personal information through masquerading as a reputable entity. This is usually done through email or websites. These emails and websites distribute malicious links that can acquire a victim's sensitive information such as account details like login credentials, and banking & credit card information.

The term "phishing" arose in the mid-1990s and actually came from the term "fishing". It comes from the analogy of throwing bait into the sea, such as the phishing email that attackers use, and hoping that someone bites it and you get a catch. The spelling goes way back, most probably influenced by an old cybercrime that used caller tones to trick people's phones. This old cybercrime trick is called *phone phreaking*.

Phishers usually use social engineering to find out more about their victims. Facebook, LinkedIn, Twitter, and other similar social networking sites are utilized to get background information that can be useful for a successful phishing attack.

The uncovering of names, job titles, and email addresses of potential victims is coined as a "pre-phishing attack". These pieces of information are vital to a successful phishing attack, giving the attacker the ability to craft a believable email that will lure unknowing victims into their trap. Most phishing attacks are launched through phishing email containing a malicious link or attachment.

Started back in the 1990's, Phishing remains to be one of the oldest types of cyber-attacks. But through the years, it has evolved and is becoming more and more complicated. More and more new phishing attacks are put to the test each year. There are a variety of attacks that fall under the umbrella of phishing. The common denominator between all of them is the disguise. Email addresses are made to look official and fake websites use foreign character sets to mask the URLs. Here are some of the most common phishing techniques:

Pharming

Pharming largely depends on Cache poisoning or domain name system (DNS) poisoning or DNS cache poisoning – the "poisoning" of a domain name system means that when someone tries to seek a certain website address, they will be redirected to another site, a fraudulent one. The fake site then tries to trick users to enter their login credentials, thus giving the perpetrators behind the fake site access to one's login information.

Spear Phishing

Spear Phishing, unlike Pharming, targets a specific individual or company. It often crafts a message that appeals to the victim. This is where the previously mentioned social engineering is put to use. Spear phishing usually involves looking at the victim's background information to make the phishing emails seem more authentic. These emails often pose as messages or requests from co-workers and executives.

Whale Phishing

If Spear Phishing targets specific individuals such as employees within a company, Whale Phishing or Whaling, on the other hand, targets bigger fish – CEOs, company board members, other high-profile individuals, and commonly, employees who are authorized to issue payments, such as someone from a company's financing department. Whaling attacks require a lot more research on the victims, to build a more genuine email, usually a business correspondence. It takes more time than the simple Pharming and Spear Phishing attacks, but the work pays off. In fact, in 2008, a group of phishing attackers sent out emails to corporate CEOs. The emails were disguised as an official email that had FBI subpoenas attached to them. The attackers were able to 10% of all their victims – roughly 2,000 successful phishing attacks.

Voice Phishing

Voice Phishing or Vishing entails the use of a phone and verbal correspondence with the victim. The most common technique in vishing is posing as a financial institution. The victim will receive a voicemail usually informing them of suspicious activities in their accounts. The attacker will then ask for the victim's account number along with their PIN, reassuring the victim that these are for safety purposes.

Users, especially employees of a certain position such as financial managers, need to be able to distinguish between phishing attacks and genuine emails. The potential damage of phishing attacks can be underestimated, thinking it could lead to just a few spam advertisements and pop-ups. Credential theft and account compromise are all results of a successful phishing attack. For more tech savvy people, it might be easier for them to distinguish between fake email attachments and authentic emails, but attackers are always one step ahead. Some phishing scams utilize JavaScript, link manipulation, and link shortening to bring victims from a safe site to a fraudulent one. Homograph spoofing is also a common phishing technique, especially during the early days of this cybercrime. Numerals 0 and 1 can be spoofed into letters O and l.

Paired with a phishing kit, these techniques could lead to a successful phishing attack. And with phishing kits easily available to cybercriminals, victims need to be wary. A phishing kit can be used, even by those with little to no technical skills. These kits can make phishing as simple as installing certain tools in the kit and sending out emails. There's no need for complicated coding and planning. There are countless of types of phishing kits available on the dark web. So, why do these kits work so well? How do veteran hackers make it easier for amateurs? How do these phishing kits work?

The first step in the phishing kit is to clone a website. The login page, however, is compromised. It is changed to point to a credential-stealing script, just like in DNS cache poisoning. The modified files are then packed into zip file and the entirety constitutes a Phishing Kit. After that, the kit only needs to be unzipped and then uploaded to the website. After which, emails that lead to the fraudulent website can be simply sent to the victims.

Phishing attacks, however, can be countered through several ways. The most obvious would be to educate users to identify phishing attacks from genuine emails and business correspondences. Gateway email filters and email authentication standards can also help verify inbound emails. Different protocols such as the Domain Keys Identified Mail or DKIM protocol lets users exclusively receive messages that have been cryptographically signed and block all the other messages. Another is the Sender Policy Framework or SPF protocol. It can help reduce the number of unsolicited emails and spam messages that enter a user's inboxes.

Another way to create another layer of defense is through a web security gateway that check requested URLs against a constantly updated database of sites suspected of distributing malware.

There are even more resources in the internet that can help a user combat phishing. There are several interactive security awareness training aids available online, and some even offer free trials. Users only need to test out which training aids suit them and their situations well. Websites like FraudWatch International also offer online users help in protecting themselves against phishing attacks by providing helpful countermeasures and software.

Chapter 14: Identity Theft

Results from a recent poll showed that a person is more likely to have his identity stolen than his car stolen, or his house stolen from. In fact, in 2017, a person experienced identity theft once every 2 seconds. That's 30 people every minute and around 16.7 million in a single year. In the same year, victims of identity fraud reportedly spent over 140 million hours in the hopes to resolve the issues. No doubt, the cybercrime identity theft is becoming an increasingly common problem.

From the name itself, identity theft is a type of cybercrime wherein a hacker becomes an imposter by collecting sensitive personal information about someone else. These pieces of information can include seemingly harmless information such as the basics; name, age, birthdate, general location, and the like. But hackers can also get actual sensitive details which includes personally identifiable information like Social Security numbers, credit card numbers, bank accounts, and even driver's license numbers. Cyber criminals can then use these pieces of information to impersonate the targeted user.

So, aside from the very general idea of "stealing your identity", what else can hackers do with a user's stolen information such as the ones mentioned above? Well, successful identity theft cases allow hackers to get a hold of money, merchandise, credit, or even services under the name of the user they're impersonating. Financial crimes are one of the most common reasons for identity theft. Once this cybercrime is successfully launched, they can commit even more such as credit card fraud, tax rebate fraud, and bank fraud. These financial crimes could cause unknowing users to be buried in debt or have their bank account savings completely wiped out.

Identity theft, however, also allows hackers to create criminal records for the person whose identity has been stolen. Imposters can give law enforcement fake identification when they're caught doing illegal things such as drug trafficking, money laundering, and cyber extortion to name a few. What's scarier is that imposters can actually commit virtually any crime without putting any risk to their own names. The blame, records, and even bail is credited to the stolen identity. Just like the numerous possibilities on what an imposter can do to stolen identity, there is also a wide range of identity thefts that cyber criminals can launch.

Cases of identity theft in general can be categorically placed under two types. The first of which is called a *True Name Identity Theft*.

This means that when hackers get a hold of a target user's personal information, they use these in creating new accounts online. Once they have a target user's basics covered, a true name identity theft can almost always be successful. Imposters can open new bank, debit, and credit card accounts, checking accounts, and even some online subscriptions.

The other general type is called an *Account Takeover Identity Theft.* In this case, the hacker uses the information he gathers to access the target user's existing accounts. Imposters don't need to create new credit card or bank accounts to access money, they use existing accounts instead. Online banking makes transactions easier for imposters because there's no need for physical interaction. Money can be withdrawn through a mobile phone and wired into another account in mere seconds. In the case of credit cards, however, it poses a problem for the imposter because usually in credit cards, any suspicious activity on the account would be immediately reported by the credit card company to the user to confirm if the activity was of their doing. When the user is notified of these unusual activities, it's only a matter of time before they realize that there's a problem. Imposters know this and have developed solutions for it, such as immediately changing contact numbers and mailing addresses when they access existing accounts. This allows the imposter to have bills and calls directed to them and not the identity theft victims.

Now that we're done defining the two major categories of identity theft, let's talk about the more specific types. Listed below are some of the most common types of identity theft committed over the years.

Social Security Identity Theft - This type of Identity Theft is on top of the list for the reason that it's the most common one. Social Security numbers are the most valuable identity asset, especially for American citizens because the government offers certain services that are exclusive to social security holders. When a social security number is stolen, it can be sold on the internet to workers who are undocumented. It can also be used to steal the services and opportunities that the government offers, as well as properties and money. These social security numbers can also be used to forge documents like credit card accounts, passports, and other important identification documents.

Tax-Related Identity Theft - Tax-Related Identity Theft cases are done using stolen social security numbers. The identity thief, using the stolen numbers, can file false tax returns with the Internal Revenue Service or the IRS. This can not only lead to financial losses, but it can also delay a user's ability to file real tax returns in the future.

Driver's License Identity Theft - This type of identity theft can be committed by virtually anyone who get theirs hands on someone else's driver's license numbers of the license card itself. Thieves can use this to run away from road crimes such as charges of reckless driving, over speeding tickets, and much more. The cards can also be sold on the internet, especially when there are people who share similar characteristics with those of the victim who had his driver's license stolen.

Medical Identity Theft - This type of Identity Theft is one of the most prominent type. It involves the stealing of medical insurance information and member numbers. When hackers get their hands on these, they can basically receive medical services under the name of their victims. The bills that the victims' health insurance providers receive will be charged to the unknowing victim, causing major financial losses depending on the medical services and products that the thief used and bought. Thieves can also get their hands on certain prescription drugs under the name of the victim, so any repercussions will be experienced by the victim, not the thief.

Child Identity Theft - Children are common targets of identity thieves because their stolen information can go unnoticed for a longer time compared to information stolen from, say, a working man who uses his credit card and bank accounts often. Identity thieves usually steal a child's social security number for several reasons. Some of which include: the abuse of the government benefits that the child is entitled to, to open bank accounts, and to ask for loans.

Senior Identity Theft - Senior Identity Theft is basically the exact opposite of Child Identity Theft, apart from the fact that an identity thief's advantage in committing Senior Identity Theft is that most seniors or old people, don't have the best security and can be complacent about who they share their information with. This is mainly because they don't foresee the possibilities of bad people exploiting the information they give out. It's not exactly easy to explain to seniors that anonymous bad people on the internet can steal their identities and abuse their benefits without even interacting with them physically.

Now that we know the most common types of identity theft, let's discuss the different techniques identity thieves utilize in order to commit all the different types of identity theft successfully.

Hacking into a database seems like the easiest way that an identity thief can get his hands on sensitive information. But hacking into databases isn't easy, especially because banks are working harder and harder to protect their databases. It's a real challenge to break the security. So, most hackers resort to some of the relatively easier ways. Two of the most common is through Phishing and Spam emails. These are both good — not in the moral sense — methods of tricking users into giving up their information. As mentioned in the Phishing and Spam sections of this book, these cybercrimes pose as legitimate businesses, financial institutions, legit organizations, and even banks, to fool their targeted users into becoming victims. They could outright ask for the information if they think the target user has already established trust, but they could also use other methods. These methods include tricking people into downloading malicious software that could steal a user's sensitive information directly from his computer, or linking users into fake websites that imitate a legitimate organization's website and prompt the user to enter his information.

According to experts, however, a large percentage of identity theft is executed through more traditional methods. These methods can be done outside of the cyber world. A common example is a practice called Dumpster Diving, which literally means that an identity thief would scour trash bins, usually in offices and banks, to steal papers that contain sensitive information. This is especially successful when people sometimes forget to shred documents that are confidential —

a common example of which is preapproved credit card papers. Dumpster diving is considered one of the easiest ways to get information that can be used for identity theft. The only con, aside from the fact that it's dirty — in both the literal and figurative sense — dumpster diving doesn't give the thief a 100% chance of getting documents that contain sensitive information.

Another old-fashioned, but still popular method is called Shoulder Surfing. How this works is as simple as an identity thief looking over the shoulder of someone who happens to be inputting sensitive information on their phones. Shoulder surfing can happen anywhere, but it's a usual scene in public transportation and crowded places where identity thieves can stand close to victims without seeming creepy. This can also happen in government establishments wherein people would fill out forms and identity thieves would secretly peek on the information that the person writes down. Shoulder surfing is one of the more old-fashioned ways of getting information from users, but it's also one of the easiest ways to get key pieces of information.

Knowing these different techniques, you might be thinking that it must be difficult to tell if your identity has been stolen. Thankfully, there are several warning signs that could tell a user that his identity is in the process of being stolen or is already stolen. Identity thieves are skivvy and clever when it comes to successful identity theft attempts, so users should be just as clever when figuring out when their identities have been stolen.

One of the most common warning signs of identity theft is unusual withdrawals from the user's bank account. Unusual meaning the transactions weren't made by the user themself. Banks might not be able to inform the user of unusual activity on their own because having successful withdrawal records under your name, means that the bank doesn't see this activity as unusual because they think it's the user, not an identity thief. The same principle applies to credit card charges on their credit reports.

Remember how the first thing an identity thief usually does is change mailing addresses and contact details? Users should always monitor the cycle of their bills. When they don't receive bills that contain their sensitive information, it might be because the mailing addresses on their accounts have been compromised, a major sign of identity theft.

Another sign, this time specifically a warning sign for Medical Identity Theft, is when a user finds medical records for a condition that they don't have. This might be reflected on records that a user submits when applying for health plans.

Another case specific warning sign is when the Internal Revenue System informs the user that a tax return was filed. The IRS usually does this as some kind of receipt, but also to make sure that the tax return was actually filed by the user themselves.

Last but not the least, when a user loses his wallet, all the cards that are inside the wallet should be reported and void. A lost or stolen wallet is usually one way of how identity thieves acquire information such as driver's license numbers, credit card information, and Social Security numbers.

So, you've checked off all of these signs and you're positive that your identity has been stolen. In the event that your identity has been stolen, here are the proper steps to take to recover from identity theft.

The recovery methods actually depend on the information that was stolen from the victim, but the best first step is to report the theft to the appropriate organization, whether it be the credit card companies, the Internal Revenue System, the bank, the health insurance providers, and the like. These organizations and companies will most likely freeze the victim's accounts to prevent further actions by the identity theft. Depending on which country the victim lives in, they should file a report with the appropriate branch of law enforcement.

In the case of a data breach, the company whose database has been compromised should find a way to recover all stolen information as soon as possible. These companies are also responsible for informing the victims about the data breach and giving them instructions on the assistance and protection the company can offer the victim.

As with all the cybercrimes listed and discussed in this book, prevention is better than cure. The same principle applied to Identity Theft. So, what should users do to prevent identity theft?

First and foremost, users should *always* be alert. Experts recommend that users should always pay attention to activities on their credit reports and billing cycles. Users should contact their credit card companies whenever bills don't arrive on time or fail to arrive at all. Credit reports should also be observed carefully, and users should always be wary of unauthorized transactions.

To avoid being a victim to dumpster diving thieves, users should always remember to shred documents that contain sensitive information as well as pre-approved credit card applications. When thieves find the latter, all they have to do is activate the credit card. And for avoiding giving identity thieves, who are also actual thieves on the street, a chance to steal a user's wallet and Social Security number, users are advised against carrying their social security cards around.

Another important tip is to educate children because they are also identity theft targets. Teach children to not easily give out information on the internet, especially in response to unknown emails. They should also be taught to be cautious when surfing the internet and be careful on who they choose to trust. Children should also be taught to report any type of unwanted interaction on the internet to persons of authority such as parents.

Identity Theft is a serious crime and it's difficult to stamp out. But when an individual is well equipped against these kinds of theft, they can increase their chances of beating the identity thieves and keeping their information safe.

Chapter 15: Ransomware

Ransomware, sometimes called crypto viral extortion, is a form of malicious software that prevents users from accessing their personal files, usually through encryption. Hackers require that a ransom be paid before they unlock and return the information to the owner. Just like traditional ransom crimes, the motive for ransomware attacks are mostly purely monetary. Unlike scams and other types of cybercrime attacks, victims of ransomware are made aware of the exploitation. They are given specific instructions on how they can get their information, files, or system decrypted with a certain amount of money as payment. Payment is often through digital currencies such as bitcoin to hide the identities of the people involved.

This type of malware can be spread through malicious email attachments, infected external devices, infected software apps, and even websites that are compromised. The malware can do different things to the device or system, depending on how it was designed. It can simply lock access to a certain device or web browser – which can be easily reverse-engineered and reopened. Hackers, however, have developed stronger versions of ransomware that use public-key encryption to deny access to files on the computer.

A Trojan horse called the Crypto Locker was one of the first ransomware attack that used public-key encryption. The malware used the RSA cryptography and experts believed that if it was implemented properly, it would be impenetrable. The malware demanded payment through bitcoin or prepaid vouchers and was active from September 2013, until May 2014 when a security firm gained access to a command-and-control server used by the attack and recovered the encryption keys used in the attacks.

Another malware attack called WannaCry infected and encrypted more than ¼ of a million systems all over the world in May 2017.

The malware used asymmetric encryption making the private and undistributed key to decrypt ransomed files impossible to recover. How WannaCry works is that it first arrives via exploit. The file is then delivered via exploit running as a service. The ransomware file is then dropped to encrypt the files or system, and then the component files for creating the ransom note are also dropped. Once all this is done, local and shared files are encrypted – and it targets 176 file extensions.

Since payments were demanded through bitcoin, the recipient of the ransom payments was impossible to identify. The impact of WannaCry was a lot more pronounced in some cases, but during WannaCry's peak, only $100,000 bitcoins were given and transferred as ransom. However, this proved to be a futile attempt because there were no files decrypted after the payment was made.

The United Kingdom's National Health Service, among the affected companies, was heavily affected to the point that it was even forced to take services offline during the attack. Other affected companies reported to have lost over $1 billion in total because of the damage. Researches, however, suggest that often the demands aren't met. It's difficult to come up with a solid statistic since several researches claim it's 70%, while other studies claim that only 3% of US-based companies paid the ransom. For the most part, however, it seems that payment does work, though it's by no means without risk. Results from a study conducted by Kaspersky Security Bulletin from 2016 showed that 20% of companies that chose to pay ransom didn't get their files back and had no accounts of their data being decrypted.

Ransomware is developing fast with mobile ransomware emerging as well, such as the Android app called Porn Droid that locks the user's phone, changes the PIN, and demands a payment of $500 to have it decrypted. Soon enough, ransomware may just find itself more prominent on the internet.

So how does ransomware work, exactly? As with everything in the IT world today, people with little or no technical background can order inexpensive ransomware a service and launch attacks with very minimal effort. This is through Ransomware kits that are easily found on black markets in the dark net, allowing cybercriminals to use complicated software with ease. These tools allow the creation of ransomware that are capable of specific things depending on the creator. When paired with the invention and utilization of bitcoin, ransoms received could be completely untraceable.

There are several ways attackers extort digital currency form their victims and the most common is through a pop-up message or an email indicating that if the amount they're demanding is not met within a deadline, the private key that will be used to decrypt the victim's files will be permanently deleted or destroyed. Another common trick is to inform the victim that unlicensed software, illegal web content, or malicious content and viruses has infected their computer, the victim is then given a fine to fix remove the malware. A similar approach is by encrypting a victim's device and then selling a product that helps a victim decrypt their infected devices.

Other ways of cyber extortion also threatens victims that if the fine is not met within the deadline, the information that the hacker has gotten will be released in public. This type of cyber extortion is used more often on influential people or big companies that will surely pay the fine, no matter how big, to keep their reputation or business clean.

Experts, however, advise against paying any kind of ransom. Although these kinds of cybercrimes can't be completely avoided, there can be ways to lessen a person's chances of becoming a victim to ransomware. One simple way is to back-up computing devices and keep software – especially antivirus software – regularly updated. Users should also be careful when opening emails with strange attachments and links on them.

More safety measures include enforcing a strict limit on when and who can access important data. This also includes segmenting the authentication systems, as mentioned in the Credit Card Theft and Fraud section of this book.

Chapter 16: Salami Attack

A Salami Attack, also known as salami slicing is a series of minor attacks that add up to create major damage. The idea is to make minimal attacks so that it can go unnoticed. These minimal attacks, however, can stack up and together can form a valuable result. Just like the meat scraps joined in a salami, thus the name.

Salami Attacks are often used in financial crimes. An attacker would steal an infinitesimal amount such as, say, a penny or even 1/100 of a penny, from a victim's bank account. If done efficiently and consistently from different bank accounts, the pennies could accumulate in the attacker's personal bank account and amount to a large sum.

A bank employee can insert a program specifically designed to steal a small unnoticeable percentage of every transaction made by the bank's customers. The amount, being so small, wouldn't be worth looking into, but collectively, the bank employee can get a sizeable amount.

Small and skillfully done modifications may not be detected in ordinary ways.

Californian Michael Largent practiced this cybercrime in 2008 when he used an automated script to open 58,000 accounts. He wrote a computer program that allowed him to push through the collection of small payments also called "micro deposits", and in result he accumulated over $50,000, one single cent at a time. He also performed the same trick to Google's Checkout service, making $8,000. In 2009, he was sentenced to 15 months in prison and a restitution of over $200,000 for the former, but he's yet to be pursued by the police for the latter antics on Google's Checkout service.

Michael Largent faced charges of wire fraud, bank fraud, and mail fraud. One can't help but wonder how the small payments didn't seem to have caught his bank's attention, but apparently it did. When his bank asked him about the small, but frequent transactions, he simply responded that the terms of service of the sites he targeted said nothing about what he was doing. Technically, he wasn't doing anything wrong. He reasoned out that he was using the money to pay off debts and not to do anything else illegal such as further cybercrimes.

This would be a strong case, but Michael Largent did the Salami slicing attacks under false names, which oddly enough included names taken from cartoons and comic books. He also utilized fake addresses and social security numbers. This led the court to charge him with wire, bank, and mail frauds.

Unlike most of the cybercrimes that were previously discussed earlier on in this book, Salami Slicing attacks aren't as easy to identify. In fact, trying to make sure that accounts are not experiencing salami attacks require a lot of time and effort. Remember, one of a Salami Slicing attack's goal is to be so insignificant that it passes through bank systems unnoticed. Rigorous box testing, or in other words, checking the entire code line by line is how salami slicing attacks are usually identified.

Users, however, can take certain steps to protect themselves from possible cases of Salami Slicing attacks in the future. One of which is to only invest in a trusted bank that hasn't been involved in frauds in the past. This might be a little difficult to find since as we've reiterated over and over again, banks are big targets for cyber criminals, but a good and trusted bank are trusted for a reason. They have security that's always updated, which means hackers aren't given a chance to familiarize themselves with the design of the bank's framework.

Trusted banks should also always encourage their clients to report any monetary deduction from their accounts, no matter how small it might be. This could help banks know when to tighten their security and what steps to make to stem out a Salami Slicing attack. Needless to say, on the side of the user, they should also make it a practice to report and openly tell banks about unusual activities on their accounts, regardless of how miniscule they might be. Users and bank clients should also be vigilant. Bank details should always be kept secure. Online banking, however, can pose a problem since bank details are stored in a database that can be hacked. So, the first advice on preventing Salami Slicing attacks stands. The safest thing to do is to invest in a trusted bank.

Chapter 17: Spam

Spam may refer to unwanted messages such as advertisements and the act of repeatedly sending a bulk of messages to a single site. They are also referred to as junk email. The most common type of spam that almost everyone who has an internet connection experiences is email spam. But spam can also be applied in other media such as instant messaging spam, online classified ads spam, and social spam among others. It has been one of the biggest problems of email users since the 1990's when it first started to gain popularity.

The term "Spam" originated from the packaged luncheon meat. The product appeared in a Monty Python sketch about a restaurant who served Spam, the luncheon meat, with everything. This led the customers to chant "Spam!" repeatedly.

Users receive spam in their mailboxes because of spambots — automated programs that collect email addresses and build a mail distribution lists. Most of spam are advertisement emails, and for good reason. Emails cost nearly nothing. Businesses and companies can advertise their products with zero operating costs, and they can do it over and over again. This makes it seem like spam is harmless, right? Aside from it being annoying, that's the extent of the damage it can do.

Except it isn't.

Spam can be used to spread viruses, trojan horses, and other malicious software. The scarier part is that these viruses and malware can have different objectives that the victim may not know about. From identity theft to money laundering, what spam may contain depends on the sender and creator's imagination.

A person who creates and sends out spam is called a *spammer*.

Robert Alan Soloway, a worldwide known prolific spammer who made it to the top ten list of spammers on the world, allegedly used millions of what the US Prosecutors called "zombie" computers to send millions and millions of spam. He was able to take over other people's domains, steal people's identities, and wire their money to his personal bank accounts. On May 31st of 2007, Robert Alan Soloway's crimes were put to an end when he was arrested and charged of 35 criminal counts. Among the criminal counts were identity theft, email fraud, and money laundering.

As proven by Robert Alan Soloway, spam can be used to conduct several cybercrimes. The most common, however, is email fraud. The advance-fee scam, also talked about in this book, is a popular scheme in spamming. Spam is also commonly used in promoting access to things that are marginally legitimate such as inexpensive pharmaceutical drugs, weight loss programs, online degrees, and odd jobs, and even online gambling.

There is also the existence of Phishing emails, further discussed in the Phishing section of this book. The phishing emails usually direct victims to a fraudulent site that asks for their login details, personal information, or even credit card numbers and PINs.

Spammers practice several techniques, one of which is the utilization of botnets. Botnets allow spammers to use C&C or Command and Control servers that collects email addresses, creates distribution lists, and distributes spam.

Snowshoe spam is also a common technique by spammers. It's the use of a wide range and a large number of IP addresses and email addresses with neutral standing to send spam. This distributes spam that won't get blocked by email service providers because the sender's email address is at a neutral state.

Another technique is called a blank email spam. Spammers send users a seemingly blank email — no body, no text. The email, however, can be armed with malware, viruses, and worms through embedding HTML codes in the email. These blank email spam can also be used to harvest email addresses for distributions lists by attacking the email server.

Spammers are getting better and better at getting their spam emails to pass through filters provided by email services. Since spam-filters search for patterns in words of an email body text, spammers included extra characters or even misspelled words in their spam emails. Some have also tried placing the text of their spam messages into picture files such as JPEG and PNG files. This lets the spam email go undetected by text-based filters. These filters by email service providers, however, are also stepping up their game — constantly developing both text-based and image-based filters to help users lessen unwanted emails enter their inboxes.

The estimated figure for the number of spam messages in the year 2011 is around seven trillion. You can only imagine the figure this year.

Needless to say, a defensive move on spammers and spam in general is to never open nor respond to spam emails. Be careful of the links that you click and always keep in mind that spam emails can carry malware through file attachments and the like.

It can be nearly impossible to stop all spam emails from entering a user's inbox, but it is possible to lessen the amount of these spam emails. Since most email service providers already have filters, a way that users can help is to report, block, and delete spam email that bypass the filters. This way, the email service provider can get a better grasp of what kind of spam email to look out for and they can prevent these types of spam email to enter your inboxes unchecked again.

Users also consider creating whitelists — a list of all trusted websites, email addresses, domains, and the like — for the email service provider to allow messages from those on the list. While this is time consuming since the whitelist must be constantly updated, the results might just be worth it.

Users who share their email addresses in public, such as bloggers or social media influencers, often use disposable or masked emails to avoid both spam and hackers to get a hold of the information their emails might contain.

Chapter 18: Online Scams

Nigeria is known for its well-developed financial, legal, communications, natural resources, stock market, transport sectors, and other industries. However, some also say it's a country with an image problem – it is known as one of the most corrupt countries in the world.

It is also home to a gang of scammers that sold a fake airport for nearly a quarter of a billion dollars. A research found that about 70% of all email traffic consists of unsolicited and junk emails. In between all the noise, are the scammers. In this section we learn about online scams; their modern-day intricacies and advancements it first began. We learn this through a journey to Nigeria, Africa.

Nigeria is known as the home of scam email. In the heart of the country is the chaotic mega city Lagos. If Nigeria is the home of scam email, Lagos is the so-called scam capital of the world. A particularly nasty form of scam that's quite prominent is the "Advance Fee Fraud". This type of scam dates back centuries. It was originally called the "Spanish Prisoner Scam", a confidence trick that emerged in the late 19th century. In this scam, a hustler convinces a victim that he is in correspondence with a wealthy and powerful man wrongfully put in jail. This "wealthy man" asks the victim to pay an advance release money to secure the release. The wealthy man will put emphasis on the secrecy of his identity and will reassure the victim that a greater monetary reward awaits the victim once the wealthy man is released.

This scam has been used and modified over time, but the key factors are kept: the secrecy of the scammer's identity and the promise of a greater reward after the transactions. This has been so widely used in Nigeria that it already has its own Nigerian criminal code: the 419 scam or the Nigerian money transfer.

One of the most outrageous scams in history used the 419 and blew it to extreme proportions. This was the most large-scale fraud ever committed in Nigeria. It involved the selling of an airport that didn't even exist, perpetrated by only 4 Nigerian scammers.

It was March of 1995 when Nelson Sakaguchi, a Director at Brazil's *Banco Noroeste*, receives a fax from Tafida Williams of Nigeria's Ministry for Aviation. Abuja, Nigeria's newest capital needed a new airport. Sakaguchi was successfully convinced to "invest" in the construction of the new airport with the promise of a $10 million commission.

Sakaguchi then heads to a hotel room in London to meet Paul Ogwuma, who was at that time the current governor of the Central Bank of Nigeria, and Rasheed Gomwalk and his wife to sign a contract. Sakaguchi returns to Nigeria afterwards to wire an advance of 4 million dollars to Ogwuma.

While Paul Ogwuma *is* a real person, he wasn't who Sakaguchi met with. In fact, all the people he corresponded with weren't who they really were. Tafida Williams from Nigeria's Ministry for Aviation was actually Bless Okereke. Rasheed Gomwalk and his wife were Christian and Amaka Anajemba. And Paul Ogwuma? He was Emmanuel Nwude, the former Director of the Union Bank of Nigeria. They were all imposters.

And they stayed imposters until December 1997 when the fraud was uncovered. *Banco Santander*, a Spanish bank, expressed their intention to take over Brazil's *Banco Noroeste*. A joint meeting regarding this intention was held. A commander from *Banco Santander* noticed that over 2/5 of the Brazil bank's totaled value as well as 1/2 of its capital was in the Cayman Islands. This led to the investigation and bank scam trial in Nigeria. *Banco Santander* still made the sale, but they weren't able to stop the inevitable collapse of *Banco Noroeste* in 2001.

The band of scammers deceived Sakaguchi for years, earning tens of millions of dollars for advanced payments on a non-existent airport. This fraud was the third largest banking scam in the world, next to those of Nick Leeson and Qusay Hussein which targeted Barings Bank and the Central Bank of Iraqi.

After several complications with the trials such as the move from Abuja High Court to Lagos High Court, successful bribery of court staff, and charges of attempted bribery and kidnap of one of the prosecution witnesses, Emmanuel Nwude confessed his guilt and received a sentence of 25 years of jail time. Along with his sentence was the confiscation of his assets. He was also imposed a fine of $10 million that was payment to Nigeria's federal government. Nwude was released in 2006 and reclaimed at least $52 million, reasoning that these assets were acquired long before the offense.

The scam went on for so long because in Nigeria, there's no sense in a man hiding his wealth. It didn't mean he was exposing his crimes because people accepted that this man was just rich. All they saw was the money, no questions were asked on how it was acquired because this was normal in Nigeria. Paul Ogwuma's impostor, Emmanuel Nwude had buildings worth 10 million dollars, houses and land worth 5 million, cars of all kinds, and a lot more luxuries.

In the time of Sakaguchi and Paul Ogwuma, the 419 scam took a lot of legwork. It required the fax, the London hotel room, and a whole lot of front. In this time and age, however, with the invention of free email services, scammers could send out a whole load of emails and cast a very wide net. They don't have to target only one person and invest all the time and resources there. A million emails can be sent out in 2 minutes all over the world. And with that, as the saying goes, a sucker is born every minute.

Hackers, scammers, and fraudsters alike can have a very, very healthy living scamming people. Victims come from all walks of life; professors, lawyers, and even teachers. That's the frightening thing: it could be you, it could be me.

As mentioned in the beginning of this chapter, the 419 scams have been modified and utilized through the years. Here are some of the most effective and downright devious of the 419 scams:

Black Money

It's basically money dyed in black that's being sold online. The victim simply has to pay for chemicals to clean the money and part of it is theirs.

Winning the Lottery

The scammer will claim that the victim's numbers came up in the lottery. They just have to pay a few piffling admin and courier charges first.

Pet Scam

The scammer would be giving away a pet that's up for adoption – completely free, just pay for transportation costs.

It's love online.

A victim matches with a scammer and it is instant love. He'd love to visit, but he has no visa and airfare. You can guess who he asks these from.

In response to the rising cases of money laundering the prominence of scamming in Nigeria, the Economic and Financial Crimes Commission or the was set up in 2003. It was also partially in response to the pressure intergovernmental task force Financial Action Task Force on Money Laundering or FATF.

Emmanuel Nwude's case was one of the first major convictions of EFCC. Since its creation in 2003, the law enforcement agency has prosecuted and convicted several high-profile corrupt and prominent Nigerian individuals. But for a population of 168 million, there are only a little over 117 convictions. That's not a very big number of people behind bars.

The EFCC, however, thinks that it's not in the number of convictions against the number of people in the country. They believe that the number of convictions that the task force has made is an accomplishment. This means that for all those times, they were one step ahead of the fraudsters, which was the key to catching them.

The EFCC website currently has a "Wanted" section on its website that displays the names, photos, and charges of several Nigerian individuals that are wanted by the agency.

But what about the rest of the world? There are also existing agencies and organizations in other countries that aim to battle online scams, but users themselves should also take their own precautionary measures to avoid being scammed. Scammers are getting increasingly sophisticated and being an unprepared and unknowing user makes their job easier, so users must protect themselves.

The first and one of the most important way to stay secure is to acknowledge that scams *do* exist. Ignorance to the fact that emails, phone calls, and websites can be scams just makes users more prone to becoming victims. A common rule of thumb is that if it looks too good to be true, then it probably *is* too good to be true.

Needless to say, it's common internet etiquette to stay away from suspicious websites. Attackers are growing more complicated but eliminating the obvious threats such as sites with sketchy URLs lessen the threats to internet users and their computers.

Along with the stay away from suspicious websites advice, another common tip is to avoid clicking on hyperlinks, pop-up windows, and attachments in emails. Emails are one of the most used vectors in spreading malware, so users should know when emails are safe to open. Viruses such as the Melissa virus can make fraud emails seem like they're from real people, so users should always stay alert.

A way to avoid viruses and malware to get their hands on a user's account is when users themselves keep their personal details secure. This might seem like a precaution that's too simple but having strong passwords that can't be easily guessed is a good step to keeping attacks at bay. Most hackers won't really do guesswork when hacking, but remember, there are still amateur hackers out there. Eliminating the possible threats presented by these amateur hackers give a user one less problem to worry about.

A less common safety tip is to *shop safely*. The internet makes things so much more convenient, and this especially applies to shopping. However, online shopping also means sharing your payment details to a website. Users should be extra careful when shopping on their phones because while it's convenient, it also poses problems and vulnerabilities. Most mobile phones lack security and antiviruses that fight off possible attacks and scams.

When we implement these steps and invest in a good security system, we can assure that we're lessening the chances of online scams fooling us. We can't completely eradicate scams, but we can be better prepared for to combat it when it comes our way.

Chapter 19: Cyber Terrorism

Cyber Terrorism is what the name itself promises: the use of the internet to cause terror. The legal definitions of what constitutes as cyber terrorism and acts of cyber warfare aren't clear since, as discussed in the last part of this book, legal frameworks that currently exist aren't exactly in line with all the cybercrimes that currently exist.

Some define cyber terrorism as the acts perpetrated by terrorist groups using the internet. An example of this could be when terrorist groups spread threats through the media, but more radical means including *actually* launching terrorist attacks through the internet. This could mean hacking into a nation's security systems and, for example, shutting down power grids. This would cause a nationwide panic and terror, and thus can be classified as cyber terrorism.

Some, however, also define cyber terrorism as any cybercrime act that insinuate terrorizing people, even if the attacks aren't outright violent. This might include the use of the usual cybercrime tools and methods such as the distribution of malware, phishing, and hacking servers and websites. These cybercrimes spread fear with the threat that they bring to internet users, so technically it can also be classified as cyber terrorism. Recent cyber-attacks have shown people that even some of the world's most sophisticated cyber-security networks have vulnerabilities that can be exploited, and this thought alone can cause fear and panic in people.

One of the famous cases of cyber terrorism is an attack perpetrated by the Pakistan Cyber Army or PCA on Indian websites. The PCA claims to be making Pakistan proud by showing the world what Pakistanis can do, saying that the world underestimates Pakistani hackers. They took control of several Indian websites, often leaving patriotic messages in place of the websites' original content. While this sounds like something that doesn't count as cyber terrorism, the

PCA revealed that their hacking activities were also in response to the Pakistan-India cyber warfare. A cyber warfare, in the name itself, is an exchange of cyber-attacks. And among these attacks some may affect not just the parties involved, but also regular people. This is similar to how the Stuxnet virus could have caused a national blackout, but it didn't specifically target the regular people of Iran. It was more likely targeting specific people such as the higher-ups in the Iranian government. So while the PCA and Indian hackers were launching attacks on one another, this can still cause terror among people because there's a possibility that the counterattacks of any of the parties can affect the regular people.

Aside from the website hacking attacks, the PCA's Facebook page also included posts by the PCA's "fans" reporting Pakistani websites that were hacked by Indian hackers, asking the PCA page to launch a counterattack. PCA also asks their followers to provide them with any website, page, or blog that contained anti-Islamic and anti-Pakistan content. The page also encourages their fellow Pakistani hackers to continue what they're doing; the page has several videos on how to hack both websites and Facebook accounts posted on its wall.

Another instance of cyber terrorism that involved a group of hackers is the 2013 hacking of popular websites such as Twitter, the New York Times, and the Huffington Post. A group of hackers called The Syrian Electronic Army claimed credit for this hacking activity. This hacker group supports the Syrian government and claimed that the organizations that they hacked posed threats to the regime of Bashar al-Assad, the Syrian president. New York Times' website, NYTimes.com, redirected users who visited the domain to a server controlled by the Syrian hacker group.

While most cyber-attacks are motivated by the financial results of these attacks, cyber terrorism attacks are becoming more and more politically motivated. Most human activities nowadays are mediated by the internet, the same goes for governments and organizations. And cyber terrorists knew this and they used it against these governments and organizations that don't fall in line with their visions and beliefs.

Unlike all the other previously mentioned cybercrimes, cyber terrorism doesn't have countermeasures for people who want to prevent becoming a victim to cyber terrorism. This crime is a large scale crime that involves the most powerful people in the world. Citizens become pawns in a power play. But users shouldn't fear, because as the hackers and cyber terrorist are getting more and more complex with their ways, institutions all over the world are also doing their best to be one step ahead.

So, how real is the threat of cyber terrorism?

First, the threat is *real*. Successful cyber-attacks have proven that lines and lines of code *can* do malevolent things. But these require a lot of work, effort, and resources. A successful worldwide attack of the same scale is possible, yes, but also improbably. There are several institutions that aim to lessen or ideally completely eradicate cyber terrorism attacks on the internet such as United Nations' International Telecommunications Union, an agency that specializes in cyber terrorism.

For the time being, the threat of a major cyber-attack that will cause worldwide damage, or "cyber-geddon", remains hypothetical than real. Experts say that what we should be focusing on is strengthening cyber security, instead of fearing what will happen when it ceases to exist.

Chapter 20: Malvertising

Malvertising, from the name itself, combines advertising and malware. Attackers purchase ad space in websites that receives huge traffic and loads their advertisements with malware - all kinds of viruses, spyware, and all the cyber filth possible. These criminally-controlled advertisements look like normal advertisements, which makes it easier for the criminals behind them to bait victims. The advertisements might look normal, but the technology that's used in them is complex and very advanced.

Tiny pieces of code is written and hidden deep within the advertisements. Malvertising commonly utilizes tactics such as the use of IFrame. These are invisible boxes that can navigate through hidden webpages without the user knowing. The IFrame then redirects the user to another page, and this page is where whatever malicious software attacks the user's computer. Sometimes information from the user's computer are sent to the servers of the attackers, giving them the chance to asses which piece of malicious software to send to the user. This all happens without the user knowing and it doesn't even need a new browser window.

What makes Malvertising a threat is that they can be on the safest sites. It doesn't matter how legitimate the sites are, the malware are hidden deep in the advertisements. In fact, attackers often piggyback on these sites in order to lure victims.

Most internet users nowadays aren't oblivious to the threats that, say, sketchy looking URLs and websites, pose. However, with malvertising, it's a lot harder to make sure that you're safe because these malicious advertisements can be found even on the safest sites. Most of them work when a user clicks on the ad, which isn't a problem for people who don't mind advertisements, and this includes a majority of people. As with all the cybercrimes, the attacks grow more and more advanced. There are some malicious advertisements that don't need to be clicked for it to spread malware - the moment a user loads a page, malicious codes from malvertising can start running without requiring any action from the user.

These days, it's becoming increasingly difficult for users to make sure that the page they're loading is safe. When a user opens a website, their browsers aren't just connecting to one URL, but several ones depending on the site. Most of the time, these URLs include the provider of the online advertisements.

So, with the tactics of hackers growing more and more complex by the day, how can internet users protect themselves from falling victim to malvertising?

The most commonly utilized tool in protecting against the threats of malvertising are advertisement blockers. These blocks those harmful and not to mention annoying advertisement pop-ups. Ad blockers lessen the chances of a user accidentally clicking on an advertisement that popped up out of nowhere.

The second best countermeasure is to have updated software. The malware hidden deep in malicious advertisements exploit vulnerabilities in software. A common example of software that can be exploited through its vulnerabilities is Adobe Flash. Outdated versions of Flash don't have the necessary patches that address vulnerabilities that were found in the past. This makes the user more prone to malware finding its way into your computer through vulnerabilities in outdated software.

Speaking of software, probably one of the simplest and most mentioned countermeasure in this book is to have a solid anti-virus software. Malvertising comes with a lot of hidden malware and anti-virus programs can help sort out and stop these different types of cyber filth from entering your system.

Due to the large amount of time users spend on the internet, even with an anti-virus program and updated software, some malware can still find its way to systems and devices, particularly those are tricky to catch and get rid of. These malwares often result in corrupted files. Which is why a good countermeasure is to make it a habit to back up data. Backing up data will lessen the amount of time a user spends trying to recover, or worse having to recreate, corrupted files.

As we've mentioned previously, most of the time successful malvertising attacks result from users clicking on the infected advertisements. There's a browser setting that sets the default to "Click to Play". This means that the browser won't run or play anything unless the user clicks on it. This is especially useful when faced with the malvertising technique that fools users into accidentally clicking infected advertisements.

Last but not the least, users should set their browsers, so they flag malicious content. Most browsers such as Google Chrome can detect the presence of malware filled sites and it informs the user. This is useful because when the browser warns the user that this certain website contains malware, the user will be more careful in clicking and browsing through the website. And aside from the presence of malware, browsers can also detect phishing sites.

All these tools put together won't make malvertising threats go away or make them less real, but these tools will make your defenses against these threats stronger and your files, system, network, and device safer.

Chapter 21: Credit Card Theft and Fraud

Cameras on ATMS and listening devices that can tell which keys or numbers are being pressed are all considered old school 20th century tactics for thievery of credit cards. Gone are the days when people invented small cameras and other related devices. The new focus of hackers? Massive data breaching.

2013 was considered the year of the full transition that moved the crime of stealing from the streets to the laptop when a group of people were able to get into the Oman-based Bank of Muscat. People from all over the world — 14 to be exact — went around different cities withdrawing 300,000 dollars a year through the withdrawal of a thousand dollars in every ATM they see. This tactic collectively gained 45 million dollars. The debit cards that were used in the operations were pre-loaded with funds. What the hackers needed to do was to simply remove withdrawal limits and send the credit card information, imprinted on fake ATM cards, to foot soldiers or cashing crews to withdraw the money.

It was coined an "unlimited operation". Much like a flash mob – operations like these require organization. And we can't help but admire the sheer complexity and elegance of these kinds of cybercrimes. Hackers are hired by organized criminals with global connections, both work together to find a victim. The hackers are then tasked to find the vulnerabilities of the victim and attack them using malicious software – or malware. Local managers from all over the world then give the information to foot soldiers or cash mules to turn digital hacking into physical money.

The central person in the operation? Hackers. When hackers sell their services to organized criminals with global connections, it produces a domino effect that will, most of the time, yield good results. In this case, credit card numbers and money. Millions and millions of money.

Credit Card numbers, however, are like vegetables and fruits. They spoil easily. Once a report is filed in the card, the card numbers would be rendered useless. So, the biggest problem for credit card thieves and hackers, would be how to get fresh numbers.

A group found the answer to this fundamental question, which led to one of the biggest data breaches in the history of America.

It was the year 2013 when the heart of American retail was struck: Target.

It began with the creation of BLACK POS by an online persona called Ree4. Versions of BLACK POS were sold to cybercriminals all over the world. In the US, the malware infected Target's air-conditioning system contractor Fazio Mechanical Services.

How it worked was that the hackers sent out several spam emails. Through this, they got inside a company that works contractually with Target. The hackers were able to malware into Target's networks. The malware was specifically designed to steal information from the magnetic stripes on the back of cards – this will help the local managers to create new cards.

The breach in Fazio Mechanical Services served as the back door to Target's entire point of sale registers in over 1,700 stores. This is a prime example of the mistakes large companies make when it comes to cyber security: network and system segmenting. The information on the credit cards should not have been accessible through a vendor-related system.

On the 27th of November, millions of credit card numbers were sent to three data centers located in Virginia, Los Angeles, and Utah over 18 days. After which, the numbers were sent to a dumping house called RESCATOR in Odessa, Ukraine. This was the biggest data breach in American retail history.

So how come nobody detected the breach?

Mainly because when big companies, such as Target, experience data breach, they fear reputational damage, so they don't allow it to go public. The usual targets of data breaches are banks and going public about losing private data is never the best interest of banks because it encourages people, and rightly so, to move banks.

The silence of major corporations means that cybercrimes pay. That is, until you get caught.

It was May 2013 when the biggest bust in the history of cybercrime was carried out. Eight suspected members of the Bank Muscat casher crew were arrested. One of which was enjoying food at a local diner when he was arrested. He was sporting a brand-new Rolex watch and was found with over a thousand dollars in his pocket. Upon investigating his home, a few blocks away from the local diner, more than 50,000 dollars was found in cash. Photos of the cash mules with their share of money were also found in the suspects' phones.

According to FBI man Tim Ryan, this was an elementary mistake. The suspects allowed themselves to let it get to their heads. They spent money on things that would really stand out, they took pictures with the stolen money, and they shared the operation through email correspondences.

In November 2013, six more mules were arrested, all committing the same mistake. This led the FBI to assume that all that were caught were just cash mules. The masterminds behind the operation remain unknown and at large.

The arrested suspects were sentenced to 7 and a half years in prison – far less that if they'd held up a gun at a robbery. This can be identified as one of the roots behind the prominence of cybercrime and cybercriminals: it proposes greater rewards with less consequences when you get caught. This, however, shouldn't lead people to believe that just because some cybercrimes don't involve guns, it doesn't mean that the cybercrimes are harmless.

Cybercrime means you're not just robbing 1 person, but you're robbing thousands of people simultaneously, all behind a computer. We shouldn't promote the notion that cybercrime is a "softer crime" compared to traditional crimes, because it isn't. At the street level, it's still a dirty business. And Albertico, the alleged manager of the Muscat Bank casher crew, is the proof that breaks the notion that cybercrime is this clean, exclusively white-collar organized crime. When you have a large amount of money, there's bound to be guns.

Albertico moved from the US to the Dominican Republic to avoid the law enforcement's eyes on him. He was in his home in the Dominican Republic, playing dominoes with two friends, when three gun men entered the home and open fired. Unlike the four who pleaded guilty and were released, Abertico was never given the chance.

Cybercrime, just like any other traditional crime, has its pay, but it also has its consequences. We all need to keep in mind that a device, moreover a system, can be compromised from a distance – physical access is not required. So, if you're playing on the defensive field for a company, developing good security is the key.

Chapter 22: Data Theft

It might have been unnoticeable, but the description of data theft has been scattered all over this book in different sections. Most, if not all, the cybercrimes mentioned in this book had data theft involved one way or another. It's basically the illegal way of retrieving data from a computer, system, or network. We've seen this in several of the cybercrimes including Phishing, Credit Card Theft, Identity Theft, and Social Engineering.

As previously stated in the Credit Card Theft and Fraud Section, long gone are the days when criminals had to use small hidden cameras. Everyone's new focus, especially the cyber world, is massive data breaching.

Data theft is the result of data breaching; the stealing of information stored in computers, networks, and systems by breaking through different databases of companies and organizations. The number of data breaches that happen in the last five years show an increasing trend. In 2012, it was a mere 470. But in 2016 it reached an alarming 1091 data breaches. This included two of the biggest data breaches ever recorded. One of which, is a successful data breach of Yahoo. The attack affected billions of people - compromising billions of people's names, email addresses, date of birth, and other information.

Another successful data breach happened in 2014, this time hackers targeted the multi-million auction giant, eBay. This attack impacted 145 million users. Information such as their names, dates of birth, addresses, and even encrypted passwords were exposed. What's shocking is that hackers were able to do this using the credentials of 3 eBay employees. According to the company, the hackers had access to these corporate employee accounts for more than 200 days. This gave them ample time to get into the company network and squeeze their way into the database.

eBay assured their customers, however, that their financial information were safe and was stored separately. Hackers weren't able to get their hands on credit card information. This doesn't mean the company didn't experience any setbacks. Aside from the reputational damage and the company financial losses that the data breach set forth, eBay also received heavy criticisms for not being able to communicate with their customers very well in such a crucial time for proper communication between the customers and the company. John Donahue, the CEO of eBay, also noted that after the data breach, the company had a significant decline in user activity. However, he disclosed that this did not affect the company's sales negatively.

Most hackers aim for massive data breaching because the results a successful data branch yields, as proven by the two examples previously mentioned, are also massive. All the information that hackers gathered could be used in hundreds of ways. Pieces of information as simple as names, birth dates, and email addresses can be used to commit even more cybercrimes. Hackers can do virtually anything with the data that they've stolen. Including using them for e-commerce, as a shield for criminal activities, and even as a business. Black markets on the dark web sell different pieces of information. Data from big companies, including credit card information and user credentials could be sold for a $100 and even more.

This section doesn't need to include a lengthy discussion on how data theft happens and the techniques thieves and hackers might use because they're already all over the book. Each of the section has something to contribute to data theft. Instead, this section will highlight the effects of data breaches and how to stop them.

Because well-known national brands and companies have been targeted, users might be thinking how they're going to arm themselves against data breaches when even these companies fall as victims to massive data breaching.

The thing is, massive data breaches happen because there's massive data to be breached. Casual internet users don't need to be scared of these data breaching attacks. However, this doesn't mean that casual internet users will never experience data breaches just because they don't own companies. Remember, the data hackers are trying to get access to be information from the consumers of a company. And the consumers are mainly the casual internet users. Which is why it's imperative that users make sure that the companies they trust their information with are worthy of that trust.

This is especially true for e-commerce companies. These companies collect information such as credit card numbers and other financial data. These companies are in charge of worrying about these massive data breaches, and it's also their responsibility to ensure the security of their customer's information.

Stopping data breaches aren't impossible, but as this book had mentioned time and time again, prevention is better than cure. Listed below are some of the countermeasures people with businesses should make.

- Secure any information clients and customers give out to the company. This should be one of the utmost priorities of the business. Paper files, storage devices, and physical infrastructures should always be secure. The business or company should also implement a strict restricted access policy. Not all employees are to be entrusted with sensitive information.
- Know how to properly dispose of data, especially sensitive ones. Companies should make sure that when they delete sensitive data, they are completely removed from the entire system. Paper files should also be shredded before thrown away to avoid falling victim to dumpster divers.
- Password-protect business computers. Employees should also have their own login credentials.
- Install antiviruses and antispyware. Malware can be one of the biggest problems businesses face because they can do an array of damages to the business, including the ability to allow hackers backdoor passage to the company's database.
- Keep operating systems and all software up to date. Installing patches immediately after release and auto-updating software

and operating systems is vital so a safe system because patches address bugs that was found in previous versions of the software. If operating systems and computer software are outdated, it's easier for hackers to find vulnerabilities such as bugs, and exploit them.

- The security control of all third-parties should be properly verified. This is especially important to e-commerce websites because they're bound to be working with third-parties which will have access to the business' computer systems and data. Businesses should know how to properly control the access of third-parties because as proven by the Credit Card Theft and Fraud case involving Target, third-parties can also become backdoors for hackers.

Through these countermeasures, businesses can build better defenses against data breaching attacks. In the following section, we move to a different kind of breaching. Instead of data, hackers breach domains.

Chapter 23: Domain Hijacking

This section will discuss how domains are hacked and how to protect domains from being hacked. The act of trying to hack an internet domain, or basically removing or taking it away from its original owner, is called domain hijacking.

Let's get to some technical definitions first. An internet domain name is the registered textual designation that says that this is yours, this part of the internet is yours. Any name that is registered in the Domain Name System or DNS is considered a domain name. The DNS service provides a global visibility for sites on the internet. Hackers, however, takes advantage of the Domain Name System's function as a phone book. We'll learn about how and why this works in the later parts, but first to understand how hacking or hijacking a domain works, we also need to understand and pull apart what constitutes a website and its domain.

A website has two parts: the domain name and a web hosting server. These two parts integrate to form a website. When a user registers a new domain name, they get full control of the domain through a control panel. The control panel will help the user point to the web server where the website's files are hosted. This is basically how a website works. When someone types in a domain and enters the website, they are pointed to the domain's web server where all the files such as HTMLs and JavaScript's are uploaded by the domain owner.

So, what happens when a domain is hijacked? Hijacking a domain constitutes taking command of the domain's control panel and pointing the domain name to a different web server. When this happens, a user who types and enters a domain name is instead taken to a different web server, and not the original web server where the original domain owner's files are uploaded.

Now let's move on to understanding *how* a domain is hijacked. For someone to hijack a domain, they would need access to the control panel of the targeted domain. To gain access to it, they need two things: the target domain's registrar name and the administrative email address associated with the target domain. When someone sets up a domain, they provide an email address that will have administrative access. If a hacker gets his hand on this administrative email address, he can have control over the domain's control panel and ultimately alter settings.

The administrative email can be found in the target domain's WHOIS data records which can be accessed through *whois.domaintools.com*. From here, a hacker can find a domain's registrar name and the administrative email associated with the domain. If the administrative email lacks proper security, it can be easily hacked, thus gaining access to the domain's control panel. By visiting the domain registrar's website and generating a new password using the administrative email, a domain can be hijacked within minutes.

So, what are hijacked domains for? Why do hackers do it? There's several different reasons but common ones include something kind of like ransomware, where hackers will ask for a payment in exchange for your domain to be returned to you. It could also be a way for hackers to steal money from you, especially if your domain is a source of income. Hackers may also use your website as a tool for phishing. Well-known and popular websites are prone to these attacks because they have a large following. When their domains are hijacked, their website can redirect that large following to a fraudulent site. Worse, it could fool them to giving up sensitive information, such as login details, thinking that they're still on the original site.

Another common reason is that the hacker may transfer ownership of the domain. In cases like these, getting back the original domain ownership can be close to impossible. The hackers can impersonate the original domain owner and take full control on the domain. These cases often require legal help.

The good news is that domain hijacking can be prevented. Understanding the reasons that lead to domain hijacking is the first step to gearing your domains and finding out how to keep them away from the hands of hackers.

One reason that can lead to domain hijacking, as with almost all the cybercrimes, is the lack of proper security. Protecting the administrative email is of utmost importance. If you lose your email, you lose your domain. Another reason could be due to security issues with your chosen domain provider. Which is why it's important to choose a trusted domain provider and make sure that there are minimal to no security issues. People, however, often opt to get private domain registration to protect their domains. This means that when hackers use the WHOIS lookup method, records of the domain and the domain owners, such as the administrative email, are hidden. Private domain registration costs more than the usual domain providers, but it's worth it because it makes sure that your domain remains secure.

Chapter 24: Hacker Groups

Before laws were made against computer crimes, a hacker can simply be someone who is a computer hobbyist. These computer hobbyists would often band together to share knowledge and resources in pursuit of their interests. However, these groups could make criminal acts. These groups could initiate cyber-attacks for fun or to send a message that could do some damage to a system. Regardless of the intention behind their actions, hacker groups can often disrupt an organization's computer networks and violate an individual's private information.

Here are some of the hacker groups that have caught government and media attention for their crimes:

Fancy Bear

It's been more than 12 years since their cyber-attacks have been detected and cyber security experts are still hot on their trails. Hacker groups have long tickled our fancies but none of them are as interesting as the ones that are actually sponsored by the governments of different countries.

The hacker group that we're referring to is none other than Fancy Bear. They have been called by many different names and aliases. Some of which include STRONTIUM, Sednit, Sofacy Group, Tsar Team, Pawn Storm, Threat Group-4127, and APT28.

Group Details

Of course, you would have to be way deep in a hacker group to actually know who their members are. A lot of what we know about Fancy Bear and their ranks is largely based on what security experts can unearth and what has been revealed on lawsuits and indictments.

For instance, the United States Special Counsel has identified and revealed that the parent organization of this particular hacker group is no other than GRU of the Russian government. In fact, they have identified two particular units in this Russian intelligence group as being the force behind Fancy Bear – Unit 74455 and Unit 26165.

Now, we know that they are indeed part of Russian military intelligence. To lend support to that claim, several security groups and companies such as ThreatConnect, SecureWorks, and CrowdStrike

The group's formation is estimated to be during the mid 2000s – any time from 2004 to 2007 in Russia. Of course, the official language of the group is Russian. In fact, they are also affiliated with another group called Cozy Bear and when these two groups work in tandem they are known as Threat Group-4127.

Why Fancy? And Why Bear?

The name Fancy Bear actually comes from Dmitri Alperovitch's coding system that has been used for various hacker groups. The word "Bear" of course was used to refer to the group's country of origin – Russia.

The bear of course has been associated as they symbol for Russia. Of course there are actual Russians who do not think this way and they believe that the bear is what foreigners have linked to their country. However, the bear has long been used in the country as a symbol and evidence is found in dramatic plays, articles, and even cartoons. Some of the literature even dates back to the 16th century.

So, why call them "fancy?" It is actually the word that refers to "Sofacy" which is a word that was found in the group's malware. It reminded Alperovitch of the song entitled 'Fancy' by Iggy Azalea.

According to a report in October 2018, released by security group FireEye, Fancy Bear is an active threat and one that is rather persistent at that. The group was also designated as Advanced and Persistent Threat 28 – thus the name APT28 came about.

The report also reveals that Fancy Bear uses zero day exploits and they mainly target computer units that have Microsoft Windows operating system installed in them. The group also targets Adobe Flash as well.

Another interesting detail about this group is that they prefer to develop their "tools" in-house. They don't use off the shelf malware and they utilize a huge maze of covert servers.

Fancy Bear Attacks

The list of agencies and groups that have fallen prey to Fancy Bear attacks have been far and wide. However, there are some who have narrowed the list down to people and groups and personalities that are deemed enemies or at least threats to the Kremlin.

Here are some of the personalities and groups that have been attacked by Fancy Bear:

- Caucasus
- Various groups and organizations in Central Asia
- Civilian agencies in Europe
- World Anti-Doping Agency
- CIA
- A French television station
- NATO
- The White House
- Democratic National Committee
- John Podesta (Hillary Clinton's campaign chairman)
- DNC
- DCCC
- And many more

X-Agent

You can say that X-Agent is Fancy Bear's most popular malware. Well, not that it is the one that they use most of the time but this is one of the tools that the group has written and developed and of course studied by security groups that try to counter Fancy Bear's methods.

X-Agent was used in the DNC hack back in 2016. This is actually the tip or end point that cyber security experts have now dubbed as the "cyber kill chain."

After the hackers have identified a target their malware will squirm its way into a destination computer. The group will then decide if this computer is worth keeping or else they move on to another one.

If the computer is in a good place to attack from, they will install persistent malware. Then they can control and monitor the computer indefinitely. Note that X-Agent has since been ported to Android, iOS, and Linux as well.

EvilToss

If X-Agent is the all-around tool that contains pretty much everything that a hacker needs, Fancy Bear has another tool that has been going around for some time – EvilToss.

This tool was built for flexibility where there is no time to inject X-Agent. It can actually load malware plugins on the fly. It does things superfast and it can be a precedent for other future attacks.

Political Targets

Perhaps one of the more well-known victims of Fancy Bear's attacks is none other than Hilary Clinton. Well, not Clinton herself actually – but more her presidential bid actually.

It has been said that their attacks have considerably damaged Clinton's campaign for the US presidency. Back in 2016 they carried out spear phishing attacks on the Democratic National Committee.

The result was that there were 50,000 emails from John Podesta's mailbox were stolen. The emails were fed to WikiLeaks as well as to DCLeaks.

These attacks are of course politically motivated hacks. Donald Trump's campaign remained untouched when all of that happened. Of course, Trump was a more congenial option compared to Clinton. Of course all of that helped to win Donald Trump's campaign.

Sports Attacks

WADA is also another victim to fall to Fancy Bear's attacks. They have leaked private doping information about US Olympic teams and other sports superstars like that of Serena Williams and the Olympic Committee for the Rio 2016 Olympics.

Fancy Bear is an active group and they are an advanced threat. It would be well to expect more news and attacks from this group in the not so distant future.

Lizard Squad

Lizard Squad is a group of black hat hackers known for their distributed denial-of-service (DDoS). They mainly operate by announcing through Twitter that they are "testing" or "have tested" the security vulnerabilities of their targets. They started out by targeting popular gaming services but, eventually, they began offering DDoS-attack services. They charge US$20 for each attack and the service interruption could last for a month.

Virtual Crimes:

August 2014 DDoS Attacks

The group first became known on August 18, 2014. They announced on their Twitter account that they have successfully taken the online multiplayer games League of Legends and RuneScape offline. On the next day, they hacked into video game publisher Riot Games' system and caused Blizzard Entertainment's gaming service Battle.net to go offline.

On the morning of August 24th, the group tweeted that they are about to undertake a cyber-attack on Sony's Play Station Network. Two hours later, John Smedley, Sony Online Entertainment's president at that time, announced on Twitter that the network is experiencing a large-scale DDoS attack.

Attack on Malaysian Airlines Website

On January 26, 2015, users of the Malaysian Airlines website were redirected to another webpage that bore the headline "404 – Plane Not Found" as reference to the loss of flight MH370. It also bore the image of a lizard wearing a tuxedo and the text "Hacked by LIZARD SQUAD – OFFICIAL CYBER CALIPHATE".

Christmas Attack on Gaming Services

On December 20, 2014, thousands of Xbox Live users were unable to connect to the service. Lizard Squad claimed responsibility for this and stated that it was merely a small dose of what they would do for Christmas of that year.

The group stayed true to their statement as, on December 24, PlayStation Network and Xbox Live went down. This prevented players from playing online and accessing the online components of some games. The gaming service networks went back online at 2:00AM on December 26.

Known Members:

Zachary Buchta

He was a member of Lizard Squad and its associated group PoodleCorp. He was charged with computer crimes and was given the sentence of three months in prison.

Julius Kivimak

He is the founding member of the group. He pleaded guilty to his charge of conspiracy committing damage to protected computers. It has a potential sentence of 10 years imprisonment but, as he agreed to work with federal investigators, the sentence was recommended to be brought down to 2 ½ years of imprisonment.

Bradley Jan Willem van Rooy

He was charged with the same crimes as Zachary Buchta. However, since he is a resident and a native of the Netherlands, he was prosecuted and tried by Dutch authorities.

Anonymous

Anonymous is a decentralized hacktivist group that gained popularity for their DDoS cyber-attacks on government agencies and institutions, governments, organizations, and corporations.

Their roots can be traced back to the 4chan raids that grew in prominence in 2003.

Their name originated from how users of the image-board website 4chan referred to the anonymous tag as if it was one individual user.

Eventually, they would be publicly known as Anonymous when they started referring to themselves as such when committing online and offline raids.

Virtual Crimes:

Project Chanology

This particular raid gave Anonymous their current popular identity. This started when Gawker, a gossip blog, posted a video that had Tom Cruise praising the religion of Scientology. The Church of

Scientology wrote a cease-and-desist for the post, stating that it violated their copyright.

This caused 4chan users to retaliate against the Church of Scientology. They organized a raid wherein the users prank-called the Church's hotline, sent black faxes, and launched DDoS attacks on their websites.

As the DDoS attacks were happening, a video was uploaded on YouTube that has a robotic voice claiming to speak "on behalf of Anonymous." The voice states that the group is expelling the Church from the Internet for the good of their followers and of mankind, and for the laughs.

The video prompted in-person protests at Church of Scientology facilities all over the globe. In these protests, protestors wore Guy Fawkes masks as stylized in the movie/graphic novel V for Vendetta.

Response to MegaUpload Shut Down

On the 19th of January 2012, the United States Department of Justice closed down MegaUpload, a file-sharing site, for violations of copyright infringement. Anonymous countered this by executing DDoS attacks on websites of various U.S. government agencies and copyright organizations. Some of the sites attacked include the FBI, Broadcast Music, Inc., MPAA, and RIAA.

Condemnation of Charlie Hebdo Shootings

In response to the attack on French satirical magazine Charlie Hebdo, Anonymous released a video stating their declaration of war against terrorists including the al-Qaeda and the Islamic State. They managed to take down various social media handles and websites that had strong links to terrorist groups.

Operation CyberPrivacy

The Canadian government passed a bill named C-51 that grants additional powers to its intelligence agencies.

Anonymous took offense to this and protested against it through DDoS attacks against various websites of Canadian government agencies.

Known Members:

Dmitriy Guzner

At the time of his arrest in November 2009, he was a 19-year old resident of Verona, New Jersey.

He pled guilty for having a role in the 2008 attacks on the websites of Church of Scientology.

Chris Doyon

He describes himself as one of the leader of Anonymous. He was arrested for a cyber-attack on the Santa Cruz County, California website.

Ghost Squad Hackers

Ghost Squad Hackers, also known as GSH, is a hacktivist group that conducts politically-motivated cyber-attacks.

They have no known members other than their de facto leader who goes by the name "s1ege".

Virtual Crimes:

Attack on Ethiopian Government

On January 2016, the GSH defaced several websites of the Ethiopian government. They claimed that this was in response to the Ethiopian Security Forces killing almost 500 students and activists.

Donald Trump

They attacked Donald Trump's website with DDoS and caused the Trump Hotel's collection website to go offline on 2016. This is in response to Donald Trump's statement during his presidential campaign that he will build a great wall on the U.S. southern border while having Mexico pay for it.

Israeli Defense Force Leak

GSH participated in Anonymous' #OpIsrael in April 7, 2016. They managed to infiltrate the system and leak sensitive information obtained from Israeli Defense Force's database.

The information leak included border patrol details, and the personnel information of Israeli Air Force and IDF soldiers.

United States Military Leak

The cyber-attacks on the Israeli Defense Force and mainstream media outlets were censored to deny attention from hacktivist groups. This caused the GSH to escalate their actions on June 2016 by uploading data hacked from U.S. Military personnel files to an onion link. The leak contains the personal information and credit card numbers of more than 2,000 U.S. Army personnel.

Attack on Banks

In February 2016, Ghost Squad Hacker worked with Anonymous in attacking the central banking system for their alleged corruption. Ghost Squad Hacker's leader took responsibility for the attacks on the e-mail server of the Bank of England, and the websites of the Bank of Greece, Bank of France, Bank of Jordan, and New York Stock Exchange.

LulzSec

LulzSec, or Lulz Security, is a blackhat hacking group that claim to cause mayhem for the fun of it. They target high profile organizations and often leave sarcastic messages to signify their involvement in the attack. The group was founded in 2011 but then has gone inactive due to most of the members being arrested.

Virtual Crimes:

May 2011 Attacks

The group's first attacks were on May 2011. They first leaked the passwords and LinkedIn profiles, and the names of 73,000 contestants of the show X Factor. This was followed by releasing transaction logs of various Automated Teller Machines in U.K. They would gain international attention when they stole user data from the website of PBS and posted a fake story stating Biggie Smalls and Tupac Shakur were alive and living in New Zealand.

Sony Pictures

Members of the group took responsibility for a cyber-attack on Sony Pictures in June 2011. The group utilized a SQL-injection attack to compromise the data of a million people. However, this number was contradicted by Sony as they said the number was only around 37,500. The information included names, e-mail addresses, passwords, home addresses, and dates of birth. Some of the data was reportedly used in scams.

Hacking a Porn Website

On June 2012, the group hacked into www.pron.com, a pornography website. They stole and published 26,000 e-mail addresses of its registered users. The information included two users registered with email addresses linked to the Malaysian government, and three users with U.S. military email addresses.

Activities on Government Systems

The group were able to get into the system of the British National Health Service on June 9, 2012. There was no leaked information that resulted from the hack. The group simply e-mailed the administrators to inform them of the vulnerability so that it can be fixed.

On June 13, 2012, LulzSec released e-mail addresses and passwords of senate.gov users. They also released the website's root directory. Although there was no sensitive information released, the group stated if their attack was an act of war. Their statement was in reference to Pentagon's statement that cyber-attacks are an act of war.

Arrested Members:

Sabu

He was considered as a founder of the group. He was arrested on June 2011 and sentenced for several hacking charges on August 15, 2011. His real identity was not released as he agreed to work with the FBI in unmasking the other members of the group. He was unofficially identified as Hector Montsegur.

Jake Davis (Topiary)

He ran the group's twitter account and conducted some of their live interviews. He was arrested on July 27, 2011 and charged with conspiracy and unauthorized access of a computer.

Ryan Ackroyd

He was one of the two operators of the handle "Kayla" in the group. The handle was involved in numerous high-profile cyber-attacks and was responsible for a botnet that had 800,000 infected computer servers for DDoS attacks. The identified operator of the handle was arrested on March 6, 2012.

Mustafa Al-Bassam (Tflow)

He was one of the founding members of LulzSec. He was in charge of security and maintenance of the group's website. The London Metropolitan Police arrested him on July 19, 2011. At the time, he was only 16 years of age.

Darren Martyn (Pwnsauce)

He was a core member of the group and worked for the Open Web Application Security Project as a local chapter leader. He was arrested on March 6, 2012 on charges of conspiracy.

Ryan Cleary (ViraL)

He was sentenced for 32 months of imprisonment for his attacks against the United States Air Force.

Jeremy Hammond (Anarchaos)

He was charged on December 2011 for a cyber-attack on Stratfor, a U.S. security company. His other charges include hacking and access device fraud.

The 414s

This hacker group consisted of computer enthusiasts that hacked into systems for fun from 1980 to 1983. They had six identified members aged 16 to 22 years old. Their name came from the telephone area code of their hometown Milwaukee in the state of Wisconsin. FBI was able to investigate and identify the members in 1983. Although most of them were not prosecuted, the members were still made to agree to stop their activities and to pay for damages. The news coverage on their actions caused the U.S. House of Representatives to introduce six bills about computer crime in 1983.

Virtual Crimes:

The 414s were able to get into the computer systems of a major international bank in Los Angeles, the Los Alamos National

Laboratory, a U.S. laboratory for nuclear weapons research, and the Sloan Kettering Cancer Center. In these acts, they simply hacked into the system as a sort of test if they could do so. If they were able to get into the system, they only played games in the computer systems.

At the time, there were no laws concerning computer hacking. This meant that the federal government cannot charge them with a crime that did not exist at the time. However, they were not able to get off without any trouble. They were still charged with harassing phone calls. Offenders can be charged by a maximum of six months imprisonment with a $500 fine for each offender.

However, the judge charged them with two years of probation and each member having to pay the said fine. During the probation, the 414 members were not allowed to own a modem. Their records were eventually purged in accordance to federal youth corrections act.

OurMine

The hacker group is from Saudi Arabia. They were founded in 2014 and hacked into the internet accounts of celebrities to advertise their services.

Virtual Crimes:

2016

OurMine hacked into various celebrity Twitter accounts. The accounts included Jimmy Wales (Wikipedia co-founder), John Hanke (Pokemon Go creator), Sundar Pichai (Google CEO), and Mark Zuckerberg (Facebook co-founder). The group only posted a tweet in these accounts stating that it has been hacked by OurMine.

2017

The group continued its social media hacking activities. This time they included the Facebook and YouTube accounts of their targets.

They were also able to leave a message on the WikiLeaks homepage on August 31.

On September of that year, OurMine were able to hack into Vevo's systems. They leaked 3 terabytes worth of internal documents that included promotional materials and office documents.

AnonCoders

AnonCoders began their hacking operations in January 2015. The group used DDoS-attacks, database hijacking, admin panel takeovers, database leaks, and website defacements for their cyber-attacks. They targeted major Israeli websites and others that painted Islam in a bad light. The group stated that these attacks were in protest of alleged crimes committed in behalf of Israel against the Palestinian people.

globalHell (gH)

GlobalHell was a hacker group that consisted of around 60 individuals. They were responsible for website defacements, theft and trafficking of personal and financial information, and illegally tapping teleconferences. Their targets included the United States Army, US Postal Service, the White House, and United States Cellular. They disbanded in 1999 as around 12 members were prosecuted and arrested while 30 were fined for lesser offences.

The Level Seven Crew

The group was formed in 1994 and eventually disbanded in 2000. They met usually online in the IRC channel EFnet to discuss the lack of security online. Their attacks are done for creating political statements and protest against governments and industries.

Their most notable year was in 1999 when they claimed responsibility for more than 60 unauthorized computer system penetrations. Their successful hackings include the First American National Bank, NASA, Sheraton Hotels, and the Federal Geographic

Data Committee. They were also able to deface the website of the U.S. Embassy for China.

TeaMp0isoN

The group was formed in 2008. They started out as a research group for computer security and consisted of three to five core members. They started their blackhat activities in 2011 which gained them notoriety. They disbanded after two of their core members were arrested in 2012.

Virtual Crimes:

Leaking Tony Blair's Address Book

The group published the address book and other private information belonging to Tony Blair, the former British Prime Minister. The leak happened on June 2011 and was claimed to have been obtained on December 2010. Blair's spokesman claimed the information came from a former staff but the group responded that they got it from the webmail server through a private exploit.

Hacking and Tapping MI6

In April 2012, TeaMp0isoN created a script to flood UK's anti-terrorism hotline with calls. They then personally called the hotline to mock the officers. The group wiretapped MI6 agents, recorded their conversations, and posted the recording on YouTube.

Participation in Occupy Movement

The group participated in Anonymous' Operation Robin Hood, which intended to take credit card information and donate to charities the 99%. The groups leaked 26,000 Israeli credit cards from Israeli banks CityNet and One.

TeaMp0isoN obtained rapper P-Diddy's credit card details and used it to donate money to charity. They also used the credit card to order pizza for anyone who requested via Twitter.

Network Crack Program Hacker Group

The group is based in Sichuan, China and was formed in 1994. They became internationally known in 2007 for their sophisticated attacks on the United States Department of Defense. The group's leader Wicked Rose claims to being paid for their black hat activities but there is no knowledge in regards to their sponsor.

Virtual Crimes:

Wicked Rose created the GinWui rootkit that was utilized in their attacks on Japan and United States. On May and June 2006, it was used to attack the U.S. Department of Defense. The rootkit is able to create, write, read, search, and delete files and directories; obtain information on an infected computer; start and kill processes, and manipulate services. The group made the rootkit available for download from the NCPH blog.

In the same year, they targeted a spear phishing attack on an employee of a US oil company. They utilized socially engineered e-mails and infected documents to obtain sensitive information. The group did these spear phishing attacks on numerous individuals but they did not state any reason as to why.

Hackweiser

Hackweiser is an underground hacking magazine and hacking group that was founded on 1999 in the United States. They first gained notoriety for defacing the websites of Sony, Walmart, Microsoft, Girl Scouts of America, DARE, Nellis Air Force Base, Jenny Craig, and CyberNanny. They are a mix of black hat and grey hat hackers. The group disbanded in 2003 after one of their members was arrested.

Croatian Revolution Hackers

The group was a black hat group known for executing DDoS-attacks, web page defacement, and data theft on their targeted websites. The group is known for attacking the websites of government agencies, big commercial banks, and mass media networks. They are famous for shutting down over 1000 Croatian websites from July 1 until July 7, 2013. At the time, they also stole data from the website of Croatian Radiotelevision.

Xbox Underground

The hacker group was responsible for the repeated attacks on Microsoft's computer network from 2011 to 2013. Xbox Underground copied log-in credentials, technical specifications, source code, and other data. It escalated to the group physically entering a building in the Redmond headquarters of Microsoft. They were found exiting the building with Xbox development kits.

They also hacked into the computer network of game developers associated with Microsoft. The game developers included Epic Games, Activision, and Valve.

Four members of the group were arrested and pleaded guilty for charges against them. These members are David Pokora, Nathan Leroux, Sanadodeh Nesheiwat, and Austin Alcala. One member, Dylan Wheeler, was able to flee to Eastern Europe from Australia. The last member Justin May was arrested in 2017 after being found with a hidden amount of cash and a new BMW in his home.

Chapter 25: Police and Cyber Crime: *Is the police prepared to deal with cybercrime? How do they catch them?*

Crime has, and will always be, a part of the society. It's a sad truth, but to be ignorant of this truth is to refuse to fight it. Crime has evolved and adapted over the years, back then they were only present in streets and required a lot of legwork, but now with a Wi-Fi connection, a laptop, and a decent knowledge of how hacking works, thousands and thousands of dollars, identities, and even lives can be on the line.

Just as the criminals are evolving and moving onto different other mediums, straying further and further away from traditional crimes committed on the streets, Law Enforcement must keep pace with criminals who are tech-savvy. A Southern California High Technology Task Force leader states that cybercrime makes up for a quarter all crimes we see. It is becoming more and more prominent that in a few years, it'll probably just be called crime.

Technology assisted crimes can't be stopped through traditional methods, so the police must keep up with the criminals who are starting to become better equipped. For Law Enforcement to accomplish this, they must have skilled investigators, up-to-date computer forensic examiners, and prosecutors with cyber-crime familiarity. Cybercriminals use secure software and proxy servers – making the method of how they commit these crimes complex. This also makes the method of catching them more complex.

As mentioned in the Credit Card Theft section of this book, companies who experiences data breaches and are victims of cybercrimes such as money laundering often refuse to go public as they fear the reputation of their companies. This, however, doesn't help Law Enforcement put their skills to the test and do their jobs.

The silence of major companies when it comes to massive data breaches, ransomware, and scams, allows cybercriminals to believe that cybercrime *pays*. And with minimal risk because Law Enforcement is often put out of the picture.

This is because cybercrimes and worse, cyber warfare, are not covered by existing legal frameworks. Because traditional wars and crimes have been a part of our history for so long, we have laws that state who is held accountable for what. There is a mandatory sentence of five years for robbery in the first degree when armed with a deadly weapon, sentences for drug distribution and trafficking, in the traditional manner, can generally range from 3-5 years to life in prison, and theft of $500 or less has a maximum of 11 months 29 days in jail. Cybercrime and the sentences that cybercriminals serve aren't as clear compared to committers of traditional crimes. Current legal frameworks stay silent on hypothetical questions regarding cybercrime, especially cyber warfare, simply because there are no easy answers.

Imagine, if a group of nations come together to infiltrate the computer systems of an enemy nation's nuclear power plant, similar to what the Stuxnet virus aimed to do. The compromised nuclear power plant, however, was luckily saved mid-infiltration by the enemy nation's own army of expert hackers. The enemy nation, as retaliates through a defensive action by means of shutting down the group of nations' power grids. Thousands, million even, of individuals and families are left with no power supply, no clean water, and heat. Hospitals in all these nations will not be able to function, putting all these lives at risk. So many factors come to play when the law begins to ask who is to blame. The retaliation of the enemy nation caused the shutdown of the power grids, but it was only a defensive attack against the allied nations who started the attack in the first place. And the retaliation was only able to work because feeble cyber security of all the allied nations.

So, who is to blame and who is to be held responsible? The computer programmers, the code writers, the creators of the software's, the engineers of the hardware, the project managers that oversee, or the commanders who make orders? No one can't really be directly blamed for large scale attacks that can constitute as cyber warfare.

It's not just the police officers, the investigators, and the companies involved that are responsible for helping put an end to cybercrime and cybercriminals. Designing an international legal framework to deter these activities will also be a useful tool in preventing cybercrimes and cyber warfare.

Chapter 26: The Future of Cyber Crime

Many generations, even those before us, have thought that they have reached the pinnacle of technological advancement. Many have assumed the golden age of technology. But if we look back, say, a hundred years back, the technology that we have now would seem like magic to people back then. Belgium has created a new technological process that manages to turn pollution in to power, increasingly advanced artificial intelligences, and the emergence of brain implants to possibly reverse paralysis are only a few of the biggest technological breakthroughs in 2017.

Technology can, with no doubt, bring us the techno utopia we all aspire.

There is a flipside, however, for all of those technologies that we marvel at and the ones that we love. In the hands of the right people, these technological advancements can do great things and can become tools to bring about conquering illnesses and connecting people.

But in the hands of suicide bombers, the future can look quite different.

Criminals use mobile phones, just like us. What they use it for, however, isn't quite the same as what we may use it for. But aside from criminals using phones, they're also building their own mobile phone networks. And there are currently mobile phone network towers deployed by the narcos in all 31 states of Mexico. They also have their own national radio communication system. Imagine the innovation and the infrastructure that these criminals have created all on their own. We often underestimate what criminals and terrorists can do with technology.

Thievery back in the days constituted going to the streets and stealing mostly tangible things like money and jewelries. In the modern days, however, thievery can constitute the stealing of credit card numbers, bank accounts, and even identities. All of which can be done without physical contact. The victim could be on the other side of the world, but still lose his identity to someone who knows his way around the computer.

Technology has made our world increasingly open and that's great, but it has also provided unintended consequences.

In 2013, Marc Goodman gave a TED-Ed talk on the future of crimes. He asks the audience to imagine a future where the massive developments in technology can make crime even more prominent than it already is. During his talk, he shares some of the events that unfolded during the Mumbai terrorist attack that happened back in 2008. According to the witnesses during the attack, the terrorists had one hand on a gun and the other on a cellphone. But perhaps their greatest innovation was that they had an operations center. The terrorists built their very own operations center across the border in Pakistan. Here they monitored both international and local stations, while also monitoring the internet and social media. All of which were done in real time. Marc Goodman also shares the terrorists' encounter with a man on the topmost suite in the Taj Mahal Palace Hotel. When he was caught hiding in his suite's bed, the terrorists asked who he was. He told them his name and said that he was a simple schoolteacher. The terrorists, of course, knew that a simple schoolteacher wouldn't simply be staying at one of the most expensive suits in the Taj Mahal Palace Hotel. So they called their operations center, who looked up the name and asked the terrorist on the ground about the appearance of the man. They then confirmed that he was no ordinary schoolteacher. Far from it, actually. He was the 2nd richest businessman in India. The next response from the operations center was an order to kill.

Imagine how a search engine, in that situation, was what determined if a man shall live and who shall die. We all worry about our privacy settings on Facebook, when in reality we have made the internet into an open book. And terrorists are using this against us.

Criminals nowadays aren't just men armed with firearms. They're men armed with technology. And that gives them power than no weapon in existence could ever offer.

In the Mumbai terrorist attack, it took 10 people, a control center, and mobile phones to terrorize a city of 20 million people. Twelve coordinated attacks that happened over the course of four days. Hundreds of people dead and more than 300 people wounded. This is what radicals can do with the openness that the internet offers.

This TED-Ed talk by Marc Goodman was given in 2013. The Mumbai terrorist attack was done 10 years ago. What technologies can terrorists create now? Or perhaps a more important questions is what could terrorists do today with the technologies that are available?

What's scarier is that it's not just about big things like terrorism. A big change in crime and criminals are also observable.

You can now commit more crime with a simple laptop. In the old days, criminals only used weapons like ice picks and guns, their targets usually just people off the street. A few years later and criminals started to rob planes, where they could target not just 1 person, but to around 200 people. The emergence of the internet allowed criminals to target more people without having to get bigger weapons. In 2011, there was a PlayStation Network outage that resulted from someone hacking the company's security. An estimate of 77 million accounts were compromised - forcing Sony to turn off the PlayStation Network. There were a million people robbed, and it happened without the need for guns or knives or trains.

It has never been possible in the history of humanity for one person to rob more than 70 million people, but it was done. And all through one security hack.

Wars have always been a part of our history. And it will, most plausibly, also be a part of our future. The wars of yesterday, however, will not be exactly like the wars we would have in the future. Alongside traditional warfare, in the future, cyber warfare may arise. This introduces a new class of weapons: malicious software, viruses, and other compromised programs. Nations can launch an attack with the press of a button and a flick of a switch, without using any gun powder.

Conclusion

In a world where technology is becoming a very big part of human life, it's important that we're aware of the risks that we're taking when we step into the world wide web. Most people use the internet without keeping in mind that they should be cautious. While the internet does offer connectedness, it also offers disconnection to reality. When someone builds an online profile, they can be whoever they want. They can wear a mask, an anonymous name, and pose as whoever they want to pose as. This disconnection to reality also makes it easier for people to cause harm because they can hide behind anonymity. This puts people at risk, because they can easily be fooled into giving up sensitive information, which, as you may have noticed, is one of the vital parts in a cybercrime attack.

We've always been warned about what horrors can happen online in school, in the office, and even in our own homes. But often we're never told why and how these horrors happen.

This book's main goal is to spread information and awareness on hackers and the world of hacking, as well as how people can better arm themselves against the cybercrimes that exist. I hope it has achieved this goal.

If you liked this book please give it a positive review on Amazon. If you feel like there is room for improvements, or if you have any doubts, please get in contact with the author at fernandoybus.com and leave a message. The author will be very happy to help you.

Thank you again for reading this book!